Enid Bagnold

Twayne's English Authors Series

Kinley E. Roby, Editor

Northeastern University

TEAS 427

ENID BAGNOLD
(1889–1981)
Photograph courtesy of William Heinemann, Ltd.

Enid Bagnold

By Lenemaja Friedman

Columbus College

Twayne Publishers
A Division of G.K. Hall & Co. • *Boston*

For my daughters—
Joanne, Linell, Kerry,
and Sandra

Enid Bagnold

Lenemaja Friedman

Copyright © 1986 by G.K. Hall & Co.
All Rights Reserved
Published by Twayne Publishers
A Division of G.K. Hall & Co.
70 Lincoln Street
Boston, Massachusetts 02111

Copyediting supervised by Lewis DeSimone
Book production by Elizabeth Todesco
Book design by Barbara Anderson

Typeset in 11 pt. Garamond
by P&M Typesetting, Inc., Waterbury, Connecticut

Printed on permanent/durable acid-free paper
and bound in the United States of America

Library of Congress Cataloging in Publication Data

Friedman, Lenemaja.
    Enid Bagnold.

    (Twayne's English authors series; TEAS 427)
    Bibliography: p. 136
    Includes index.
    1. Bagnold, Enid—Criticism and interpretation.
I. Title.   II. Series.
PR6003.A35Z66   1986   828'.91209   86-11988
ISBN 0-8057-6922-6

Contents

Preface

Enid Bagnold was an English author and playwright with a zest for life and a love of language. She began her career as a poet, publishing a book of poems in 1917; and then for the next sixty years of her writing career she concentrated her efforts, first on the novel and then on the theater. Her works include one nonfiction book about her experiences in a hospital in World War I and five novels, in addition to a children's book and an autobiography, her crowning achievement. She wrote eight plays, among them an adaptation of her novel *National Velvet.*

This book, the only full-length study of Miss Bagnold and her work, presents her as a stylist, an experimenter with form and technique. One sees that her writings, especially the novels, are strongly autobiographical and that in characterization and purpose there are major differences between the novels and the plays. Her writing reveals a talent for the use of words, a fondness for aphorisms and elliptical utterances, and a flair for wit and humor. Although the plays are not as strong as the novels, Bagnold's sense of drama is impressive and cannot be ignored.

Her artistic life span was long, and she experienced a world undergoing tremendous changes not only in literature but in scientific inventions, shifting attitudes, values, and the influence of two world wars. She knew as friends and acquaintances many of the important men and women of the twentieth century: writers, theater people, government officials, and foreign dignitaries.

A touching commentary about her work comes from the obituary in the London *Times* of 1 April 1981: "As a writer, Enid Bagnold's success was perhaps greater with the public than with critics, because versatility and craftsmanship made her suspect to the latter, while ensuring her several large audiences—one for *Serena Blandish,* another for *National Velvet,* and a third for *The Chalk Garden*—which rarely came in contact with one another. She never published with the compulsive frequency of the professional writer and never wrote for a living, yet no professional took more care over the sharpening and refinement of language than she."[1]

Lenemaja Friedman

Columbus College

Acknowledgments

I wish to thank the staff of Columbus College Library, especially Callie McGinnis, Sharon Self, and Frederick Smith, for the special assistance given me in my research, and I thank also the staffs of the University of London Library and the British Museum Newspaper Library.

In addition, I thank my colleagues and my family for their cooperation when I needed it, and Audrey Wolfe and Jackie Sizemore for their help in typing the manuscript.

Excerpts from *A Private View* by Irene Mayer Selznick, © 1983. Reprinted by permission of Alfred A. Knopf, Inc.

Excerpts from *The Letters of Evelyn Waugh* edited by Mark Amory. © The Estate of Laura Waugh, 1980. Reprinted by permission of Ticknor & Fields, a Houghton Mifflin Company.

Excerpts from *The Letters of Virginia Woolf,* volume II, © 1976 by Quentin Bell and Angelica Garnett. Reprinted by permission of Harcourt Brace Jovanovich, Inc.

Excerpts from *The Letters of Virginia Woolf,* volume IV, © 1978 by Quentin Bell and Angelica Garnett. Reprinted by permission of Harcourt Brace Jovanovich, Inc.

Chronology

1889 Enid Bagnold born in Rochester, Kent, England, 27 October, daughter of Arthur and Ethel Alger Bagnold.

1896 Brother Ralph born.

1899 Family moves to Jamaica where her father is in command of the Royal Engineers.

1902 Family returns to England.

1903 Enid goes to Prior's Field, a school run by Mrs. Leonard Huxley.

1906 Brief sojourn in finishing schools in Germany and Switzerland. School in Neuilly (Paris), France.

1907 Back home in Warren Wood. Debut at Royal Military Academy, Woolwich.

1909 In London, an art student of Walter Sickert.

1913 Meets Frank Harris. Works as his editorial assistant on *Hearth and Home*. Later on staff of *Modern Society* with Harris.

1914 Back home in Woolwich. England declares war on Germany, 3 August.

1916 Working as V.A.D. in Royal Herbert Hospital.

1917 *The Sailing Ships and Other Poems*.

1918 Publication of *A Diary without Dates* causes her dismissal from the hospital. Volunteers as a driver for French Army with other Englishwomen.

1920 Marries Sir Roderick Jones, owner and director of Reuter's News Agency. *The Happy Foreigner* published, her first novel.

1924 *Serena Blandish, or The Difficulty of Getting Married,* under pseudonym of a Lady of Quality.

1929 S. N. Behrman's version of *Serena Blandish* opens on Broadway 2 January for 93 performances.

1930 *Alice and Thomas and Jane,* written for her children.

1933 Makes exploratory trip to Germany.

1935   *National Velvet* (England and America). Translation of *Alexander of Asia* by Princess Marthe Bibesco.

1938   *The Squire* (also published as *The Door of Life*).

1941   *Lottie Dundass,* her first play, opens in California. Roderick resigns from Reuter's.

1943   *Lottie Dundass,* produced at the Vaudeville Theatre, London, on 21 July for 147 performances.

1944   *National Velvet* made into Metro-Goldwyn-Mayer film.

1946   *Poor Judas* produced at Bradford Civic Theatre, Bradford, England. Play adaptation of *National Velvet,* Embassy Theatre, London, 23 April.

1950   *Lottie Dundass* and *National Velvet* adapted into radio plays for Theatre Guild on the air.

1951   *Poor Judas* awarded Arts Theatre Prize. Last novel, *The Loved and Envied* (New York and London). *Lottie Dundass* and *Poor Judas* published as *Two Plays;* republished as *Theatre* by Doubleday.

1952   *Gertie* opens at Plymouth Theatre, New York, for five performances; produced again as *Little Idiot,* 10 November at Q Theatre, London.

1954   *The Girl's Journey* (Doubleday), includes *The Happy Foreigner* and *The Squire.*

1955   *The Chalk Garden* opens on 26 October at the Ethel Barrymore Theatre, New York.

1956   *The Chalk Garden* opens at the Haymarket Theatre, London, for 658 performances.

1960   *The Last Joke* opens 28 September, Phoenix Theatre, London, for 61 performances.

1962   Death of Roderick Jones.

1964   *The Chinese Prime Minister* opens at Royale Theatre, New York, for 108 performances. *The Chalk Garden* is made into a film.

1965   *The Chinese Prime Minister* opens 20 May at Globe Theatre, London.

1968   *Call Me Jacky* opens at Oxford Playhouse on 27 February.

1969 *Autobiography: From 1889* (London); republished as *Enid Bag-nold's Autobiography* (Boston).

1970 *Four Plays* (London) includes *The Chalk Garden, The Last Joke, The Chinese Prime Minister,* and *Call Me Jacky;* republished in Boston in 1971.

1976 *A Matter of Gravity* (revised version of *Call Me Jacky*) opens at Broadhurst Theatre, New York, with Katharine Hepburn.

1980 *Letters to Frank Harris & Other Friends.*

1981 Dies on 31 March.

Chapter One

The *Autobiography*

The Beginnings

Enid Bagnold was born in Rochester, Kent, on 27 October 1889. She was the daughter of Major Arthur Henry Bagnold of the Royal Engineers and Ethel Alger, both the products of prominent families. Several members of Major Bagnold's family were career army officers; his father had been a general in the Honorable East India Company. Ethel Alger's family were propertied, with connections in politics; her father had been elected mayor of Plymouth three times.

Enid claims that she grew up a spoiled child, the pride of her mother and father, a rough little girl and sometimes a bully. Her sole reign ended at six, however, when brother Ralph was born.

Major Bagnold's engineering assignments caused the family to move several times in the area of the south of England. Then, when Enid was nine, her father received a command in Jamaica. He sailed ahead and the family followed soon thereafter in a cargo ship. The crossing was so stormy, apparently, that Enid developed a lifelong wariness of the sea.

Jamaica was a tropical wonderland, awakening her artistic and poetic impulses. Never had she seen such beauty. She speaks in the *Autobiography* years later of the importance of this experience: "The day we neared Jamaica an inner life began. It must have, for I never remember anything earlier of ecstasy or admiration for nature. Beauty never hit me until I was nine. . . . This was the first page of my life as someone who can 'see.' It was like a man idly staring at a field suddenly finding he had Picasso's eyes. In the most startling way I never felt young again."[1]

To escape the heat of Kingston, Major Bagnold rented a large historic manor, a former coffee plantation in the Blue Mountains. The house and environment were so impressive that even after sixty years Enid Bagnold clearly remembered details of their home. Her memories included childhood naughtiness and fear of the bats that inhabited the house.

During this time she developed a love for horses, and as they had no riding animals, she cut out pictures of horses from old magazines and pretended she was riding, galloping through the coffee bushes. When she was older, she was allowed to ride on a donkey and given the freedom to wander over the mountainsides.

She spent more time writing than reading. At night she knelt in bed and wrote poems. Then, her father, afraid that the activity might result in insomnia, made her promise to write only three nights a week.

A governess had accompanied the family to Jamaica, and Enid evidently spent several hours a day in formal study. When a change of governesses came, she was delighted, as the new teacher allowed more freedom and demanded less schoolwork. At this stage the young Enid may well have been the prototype of the headstrong Laurel in *The Chalk Garden,* a terror for the household staff. Aside from her younger brother and the daughter of an army doctor whom she saw periodically, she had no companions.

To School in Various Places

Three years later, on 28 March 1902, the Jamaica idyll was over, and the Bagnolds sailed for England and a new assignment. They had been home for one year when it was decided that Enid should enter Mrs. Leonard Huxley's boarding school, Prior's Field near Godalming. Mrs. Huxley was the mother of Julian, Trevor, and Aldous.

Enid loved the school. On Sundays sometimes she saw Mrs. Huxley's sons. Later she and Julian wrote poems and sent them to each other; he was attending Eton at the time. She was impressed with Mrs. Huxley, recognizing her as a "great woman." As a result of Mrs. Huxley's reading aloud to her pupils in the evening, Enid became as enamored of words as she had been earlier with horses. There were private interviews with Mrs. Huxley now and then, not to discuss literature but because Enid had been sent for punishment. Once she had climbed down the pipes outside the lavatory to wander off and sleep in the woods, but on that occasion Mrs. Huxley was quite lenient and that incident, like others, was forgiven and forgotten.

To be good at sports and to be popular were more important to Enid at this stage in her life than good marks. She had a lively personality, was a natural tomboy, and enjoyed being the center of attention. She was clever but felt compelled to act the clown, partly to compensate for her chubbiness.

When Enid was fifteen, she and the other girls were given the challenge of writing a verse-essay. She composed a long, five-page poem with choruses and several changes of metre. On the last day of the term during festivities the winner was announced. Mrs. Huxley spoke of the poetry experiment and of the one poem that was outstanding, naming Enid as the author. The girls had had no indication of her poetic talents and reacted in amazement. The class clown was also the class poet.

During the holidays Mrs. Huxley took her to see William Butler Yeats in London. At an evening party he told her that if she wanted to be a poet, to do creative or imaginative work, she must not be concerned with politics or welfare or even people's living conditions, but with their hearts and minds and what they were.

Shortly after the beginning of the next term Mrs. Huxley became ill and died. The school was never the same for Enid afterwards although the new headmistress gave her special privileges, removed her from the regular curriculum, and tried to teach her Greek. Her interests were changing, however, and she became involved with current events, the rights of women, Mrs. Pankhurst, and socialism.

When her course of studies was finished and her years at Prior's Field were over, it was time to go abroad to learn other languages. She was now seventeen. First, she spent three months at a German school in Marburg. Not very happy there, she enrolled in a small school in Lausanne, presumably to learn French, but at the end of the first week an incident occurred that so angered her that, with the common consent of all, she left.

Her next trip was to Paris, to enter an expensive school at Neuilly. She was exceedingly happy during this year, 1906–1907, discovering the French theater, Sarah Bernhardt, and Napoleon. The French language and literature were a joyful challenge, largely as a result of her devotion to a Mademoiselle Ruth Charpiot who read Verlaine aloud to her.

Home in Woolwich: The Fledgling Writer

At the end of the year Enid returned home to Woolwich. Several years earlier her father had been made Chief Superintendent of Building Works at Woolwich Arsenal and had bought the house called Warren Wood, where Enid continued to live intermittently until she was thirty. She describes herself in 1907 as "the great gosling come home. Awkward, clever, bubbling, in touch with life but not with graces, mad about herself, furious with her face, not well dressed, unable to dance . . ." (A, 54); but her family loved her and took pride in presenting her to society.

The positive quality that Enid had, the confidence, the exuberance seemed to be obvious to all who came to know her. She credits her mother with giving her this belief in self which remained throughout life. Only the theater, she maintained, had shaken her confidence.

At eighteen she attended her first ball, a "coming out," at the Royal Military Academy at Woolwich. The Royal Engineers were of the top group at the academy. Her father was one and so was brother Ralph later on; she had determined, however, that she would never marry a soldier. She wanted more than the typical married quarters in India or Egypt; she yearned instead for an elegant, sophisticated social life with the brilliance of title and money.

The question was, what was she to do now? She had no desire to learn the housewifely arts of cooking or gardening or sewing, all those chores which twenty years later, as a contented wife and mother, she delighted in. It more suited her "emancipated" disposition to remain, in one sense, the tomboy, to realize that like her father, she also had a curiosity about mechanical objects. She appreciated his genius for invention and enjoyed watching him work. She took her bicycle apart and had difficulty getting it back together, but when she took apart her typewriter, she did as her father suggested, numbered the pieces on a board and then successfully reassembled it.

At the same time her social life continued. She was attending dances, and soon thereafter received the first of several proposals of marriage, none of which she considered seriously. Then she began to write poetry again, and her literary life became important. She received several rejections before a weekly paper called the *Iron Age* accepted a poem. Major Bagnold decided now that if his daughter were to continue to live at home and become a writer, she would need her own study; therefore, he prepared a room in a turret at the top of the house where she could enjoy the privacy a writer needs. As she says in the *Autobiography,* "It was my first 'Tower Room.' . . . My life simply thundered in that room. It took on a momentum that has never stopped; . . . bit by bit I became the disciplined writer" (A,

81); in addition to writing, she became interested in art and for a time took drawing lessons at the Blackheath Art School. Sketching, she found, was also one of her talents; later she was to illustrate her first book *A Diary without Dates* and often included sketches in letters to friends.

London: The Duckling Becomes a Swan

At a neighborhood garden party she met Dolly Tylden, daughter of the general in command of the garrison. They became friends, sharing a desire to experience "life." The vivacious Miss Tylden suggested that they go to live in London, and Enid, now nineteen, agreed but first had to obtain her father's permission. Finally it was determined that she would apply to study art at the drawing school of Walter Sickert in London, during which time she was to receive an allowance of seventy-five pounds a year.

They found a flat in Rectory Chambers, Lower Church Street, in Chelsea. Luckily the general's daughter had a gift for making friends, and they became part of an artistic group which included Lovat Fraser, Gaudier-Brzeska, Kenneth Hare, and Holdane Macfall. Katherine Mansfield had been part of this group earlier and had just returned to London from New Zealand; Mansfield, one year older than Bagnold, had already begun to publish short stories and poems.

Bagnold was fascinated with London; she explored the city with Lovat Fraser, enjoying her present freedom, and fortunately she was accepted as a student by Walter Sickert. She achieved a degree of success, for two of her drawings were presented at an exhibition and one was even mentioned in the *Times*. Besides taking art lessons, she helped Sickert prepare the copper plates for his etchings. A Walter Sickert drawing of Bagnold was published in the *New Age* (1913).

Walter Sickert became a good friend; and for a time they both joined Ralph Hodgson, then the editor of C. B. Fry's Magazine, and a select group of others at a lunch table at a well-known vegetarian restaurant, although none of them was a vegetarian. Hodgson had chosen the restaurant because the management kindly allowed his dog to sit on a chair beside him.

Bagnold had begun to write poetry again. Two poems were published in July 1917, one in the *Nation* and the other in the *New Statesman;* in the following year Heinemann published her poetry collection, *The Sailing Ships and Other Poems*.

Enid's allowance was not adequate and getting a job seemed the answer, but where? At a bookstore in St. Martin's Court, a gathering place for young writers and painters (including Katherine Mansfield and John Middleton Murry), Bagnold met Frank Harris. Harris (then about fifty-four) had become editor of a publication called *Hearth and Home;* for this, he needed a staff and offered her a job which she gladly accepted. In the next few months a group of admiring persons gathered around Harris, but, gradually discouraged by his displays of ego and temper, they disappeared, and she found herself the only follower. He was, she felt, an extraordinary man. Also, she was now being courted by him with lunches at the Savoy and was meeting an older group of established writers.

In the course of her journalism duties Bagnold was sent on interviews and was writing articles. For a story on young women writers, she contacted Rosalind Murray and Katherine Mansfield. In June 1912 Katherine Mansfield and John Middleton Murry had become coeditors of *Rhythm,* a publication which lasted only until March of the following year. Bagnold's first big interview was with Mrs. Annie Besant and two young Indian boys. Bit by bit her literary work began to take precedence and the art work became secondary.

Soon thereafter Frank Harris left his editorship and bought a periodical called *Modern Society.* Bagnold maintains that she did the bulk of the work for thirty-five shillings a week, which she had to ask for each week; to complicate matters, the working relationship became a personal one, and Frank Harris became her first lover.

Their friendship became strained after he received a Contempt Citation during a routine court appearance and was sent to prison. In February of 1914 she found herself frantically contacting such famous writers as Bernard Shaw and Max Beerbohm to provide enough copy to help fill the paper. Shaw refused, but Beerbohm created a drawing of himself and Frank Harris; he made her promise, however, that it would not be used as a cover or be made into a poster.

She visited Harris in the prison in Brixton and gave him an account of her activities; in the course of the visit he promised not to violate Beerbohm's conditions. Yet, within a few hours and unknown to her, he sent instructions to have the drawings made into posters. The deed was discovered when she found the roll of posters being delivered to the office. She felt compelled then to contact Beerbohm and tell him what Harris had done. Together they drove to the office, collected the posters, and went on to the printers to collect the block.

Next, they drove down to the river and threw everything (except one poster for herself) into the river. This incident supposedly marked the end of the relationship with Frank Harris, but for several years thereafter she corresponded with him, and her letters give evidence of a deep fondness.

Back in Woolwich: A New World and a Serious Career

Now Bagnold moved home again. She had been for some time going back to Woolwich on weekends; therefore strong family ties were never broken. She tried at first to write a novel about Frank Harris but never finished it. In her tower room she kept a disciplined schedule of writing; friends came from London to visit and she was content. Then the Baroness Catherine d'Erlanger bought Falconwood, a neighboring estate, where people of fashion and wit crowded in to the numerous parties. In the *Autobiography* Bagnold quotes Charlotte Brontë as saying, "I like high life. I like its manners, its splendours, the beings which move in its enchanted sphere" (*A,* 137). She agreed and was anxious to see these splendid people in the "high life." Soon thereafter she met the baroness (the prototype of the Countess Flor di Folio in her novel *Serena Blandish*), and becoming one of the select group brought a big change in her life. The society world presented a challenge that suited her. Here were people speaking and laughing in many languages but behaving as one big family.

Meanwhile, Bagnold the writer was making mental notes, analyzing, storing materials for future use. She found, however, as she wrote in the *Autobiography* at age seventy-nine, that she did not wish to include material that had already been used in her novels and plays. Her created world is based heavily on the situations and the people of her life. She recalled that Cyril Connolly had said of Rosamund Lehmann's book *The Swan in the Evening,* that "She had 'processed' parts of her life already in her books and that therefore they couldn't come into her autobiography" (*A,* 143). This is true also in Bagnold's case; yet one finds that she is not consistent in providing background information. Whereas she includes several pages on the models of the main characters of *Serena Blandish* (in which she herself is not a main character), she says very little in the *Autobiography* about her Voluntary Aid Detachment nursing experiences in the wartime hospital upon which *A Diary without Dates* is based, or about her experiences as a driver for the French army upon which *The Happy Foreigner* is based. *A Diary without Dates* is an impressionistic account of a real situation but lacking the details of time and place or the identification of the speaker. Lack of detail regarding the central character is typical also of the impressionistic technique of *The Happy Foreigner*.

When on 3 August 1914 England declared war upon Germany, Bagnold's nineteen-year-old brother Ralph joined the army; the d'Erlangers closed up Falconwood and restricted their social life to London, and she took classes for a V.A.D. certificate to become an auxiliary nurse. Whether people were trained or not, they were urged to volunteer their services to the big military hospital (the Royal Herbert) close by. She worked during the week as a V.A.D. nurse and on the weekends spent time at Catherine d'Erlanger's house. There she met Prince Antoine Bibesco, first secretary of the Roumanian Legation, with whom she fell in love.

With Antoine and his neurotic brother Emmanuel (an important character in her play *The Last Joke*) Bagnold made car journeys about the countryside, she doing most of the driving. When Emmanuel commited suicide, the shock to Antoine with the ensuing depression ended the love affair although they continued to be friends for the remainder of his life. Antoine is undoubtedly the prototype of Julien in *The Happy Foreigner*.

While Bagnold worked at the Royal Herbert, she kept a diary of the incidents that made a deep impression on her. Antoine was the one who said that she should make it into a book. She sent the finished manuscript to Heinemann Publishers, but her good friend Desmond MacCarthy, theater critic and essayist, who was reviewing books for them, lost it on a bus. The only other copy, but without the drawings to accompany it, was in the possession of Ralph Hodgson in a military unit in eastern England. Luckily, she was able to retrieve this copy.

When *A Diary without Dates* was published (1918), the hospital fired her. She had been critical of the sisters (the nurses), of their less-than-compassionate behavior, lack of sensitivity, and sometimes distorted sense of values; needless to say, the administration did not appreciate her candid view of hospital conditions. The newspaper the *Daily Mail* reported the incident, especially as a recent hospital scandal in Rouen had made the event newsworthy. Bagnold thought that Desmond ought to have reviewed the book since he was responsible for losing it. One must appreciate both her wit and her ear for conversation as she remembers the dialogue with Desmond. He had said no, apparently:

> . . . "I give you my friendship," he said, "instead."
> "Suppose I would rather have your review?"
> "You can't undo friendship and I don't review my friends."
> "But suppose I was Shelley or Shakespeare?"
> "But you aren't." (*A,* 170)

She has a flair for the dramatic, obviously, and the ability to laugh at herself. In regard to Bagnold, MacCarthy, and the book, a letter from Virginia Woolf to her sister Vanessa Bell provides an entertaining highlight to this situation. Miss Woolf did not know Enid Bagnold but believed the worst of her. The letter, therefore, is ironic in that it not only gives a false picture of Bagnold but also indicates a certain lack of charity in Woolf's own personality. She says:

Well, old Desmond (MacCarthy) turned up the other day, and I have scented a minute romance for you—I'm afraid only a figment, but better than nothing. Did you ever meet a woman called Enid Bagnold—would be clever and also smart? Who went to Ottoline's parties, and now lives at Woolwich and nurses soldiers? "That disagreeable chit?" Yes, that is my opinion too. But she has evidently enmeshed poor old Desmond. She has written a book, called as you can imagine *"A Diary Without Dates,"* all to prove that she's the most attractive, and popular and exquisite of creatures—all her patients fall in love with her—her feet are the smallest in Middlesex—one night she missed her bus and a soldier was rude to her in the dark—that sort of thing. Desmond insists that I shall review it in the Times. First he writes a letter; then he comes and dines; then he gives me the book; then he invites me to lunch with a Prince Bibesco, who is apparently one of Bagnold's lovers; then he writes again—and every visit and letter ends with the same command— for God's sake review this book!

So far I have resisted; but I don't know that Desmond's charms won't overcome me in time. The Roumanian Prince too has the most exquisite voice. To charm me further, Desmond rang him up, and I listened—but the appalling thing is that Desmond is now, whether from drink, Bagnold or bankruptcy in such a state of dissolution that one has to be very careful what one says. . . . Bagnold has said to him "Now I won't kiss you" (or whatever it is they do) "until you've got my book reviewed in the Times." Bagnold has him in her toils.

The question is, am I a match for Bagnold? You would be, of course, but then I'm so susceptible. Bagnold paints too.[2]

Although Virginia Woolf came to know and like her better in later years, she admitted envy of Bagnold's ability to attract people and her opulent life-style. Bagnold, on the other hand, had always admired Virginia Woolf's genius. Once when H. G. Wells was staying with her family at Rottingdean, he argued that *beauty* didn't matter while *sense* did and that beauty was meaningless. To refute his argument she rushed for her copy of Woolf's *Orlando,* which opened readily to a favorite descriptive passage, the ice scene on the Thames, but by the time she returned, Wells was already involved in another conversation with her husband Roderick.

H. G. Wells was one of the many friends that she had acquired over the years. They had met some time before 1914. She had been warned about his reputation with the ladies but apparently was not threatened by what she heard. Wells had had romantic involvements with both Dorothy Richardson and Rebecca West, but Bagnold claims that she was never one of his attachments. He seemed to appreciate her wit and vivacity and also admired *A Diary without Dates* enough to mention it favorably in a review. He said: "Nowadays of course nobody reads the books of the generals and admirals and politicians of that time, and all the official war histories sleep the eternal sleep in the vaults of the great libraries, but probably you have all read one or two such human books as Enid Bagnold's 'Diary Without Dates,' or Cogswell's 'Ermytage and the Curate'.". . (*A,* 171–72).

Just as the war was ending Enid Bagnold volunteered as a driver for the French Armed Forces Command. Several Englishwomen were already drivers in France. She now had the distinction of being the first woman to enter Verdun with the French Army in 1918. These experiences served as the basis for her first novel *The Happy Foreigner* (1920).

Marriage: Life as Lady Jones and Success as an Author

Within the two years before she met Sir Roderick Jones, Enid Bagnold had been engaged twice. Now she was thirty; Roderick was forty-two, and the president of Reuter's News Agency. She did not take his proposal seriously and had gone on a special mission to Vienna with the Quakers, a postwar relief project. During her two months' stay she was bombarded with letters and cables from Jones and finally tickets to meet him in Paris. She couldn't resist. He immediately bought the ring and they were engaged. In the summer of 1920 they were married in Chelsea Old Church; their honeymoon was far from private as it consisted of a journey with one hundred editors to an Imperial Conference in Canada.

Bagnold had established a rule from the beginning of their marriage that she would spend three hours each day writing. Aside from that, she was to manage a household of servants and, in time, more than one house. Suddenly she found herself with the pleasures and problems of being wealthy, of being Lady Jones, of being expected to entertain the guests of Reuter's. Cutmore, the head butler, and the prototype of various butlers in her novels and plays, remained with the family for twenty-nine years. Eventually, besides Cutmore, there were nine indoor servants in addition to nurses, gardeners, a chauffeur, and a groom for the horses. In the next few years four children were born to the Joneses. Laurian came first in 1921 and then Timothy, next Richard, and finally Dominick (Tucker).

Finding time to write became increasingly difficult, for she was the manager, and if writing hadn't been as important as it was, she would not have continued the daily routine during these busy family years. As in *National Velvet,* the children took part in riding competitions. Laurian, like the fictional Velvet Brown, had "horse-passion," and the whole family became involved.

The house at 29 Hyde Park Gate had been acquired as very suitable for entertaining. Roderick had insisted that the dining room be large enough to seat twenty-eight. The guests of honor were of varying degrees of importance and of many nationalities: once six Japanese princes were entertained. On these occasions a local guest list had to be made up. When the guests accepted, their titles had to be listed properly, and table etiquette demanded that name cards be printed and menus be handwritten.

Bagnold felt uncomfortable often in the role of Lady Jones and saw the dinner parties as chores she needed to do for her husband; she could not enjoy them because her days were too full. A special writing room was built into a corner above the drawing room.

Reuter's had many crises and she found that night telephone calls always brought bad news. The news agency was a vast network of people spread over thirty-eight countries. In her *Autobiography* she relates tales, mostly humorous, about experiences in Geneva and elsewhere in the world with Reuters' personnel.

The country house the Joneses bought was in Rottingdean; North End House it was called. All in all, Roderick Jones bought four houses on opposite sides of the village green. Now they began to entertain in Rottingdean, with regular trips between there and London.

In 1920, the year of her marriage, Bagnold had published *The Happy Foreigner;* and in 1924, under the pseudonym of a "Lady of Quality" she had published the novel *Serena Blandish.* When her father was shown the manuscript before publication, he forbade her to use her own name. He claimed that he wouldn't be able to show his face in his London club if his friends knew that his daughter had written the book.

In 1930 she published the children's book *Alice and Thomas and Jane* with illustrations by herself and Laurian. This work deals with the adventures, actually fantasies, of three children living in Rottingdean. During the escapades, Alice stows away in an airplane, and Thomas wanders off to Dieppe in a series of comic events until his mother comes to rescue him. Much of the humor and the irony here develop as one realizes that the bizarre activities of the children's world are going unseen and unsuspected by the adult world, and the young people are extraordinarily ingenious.

In 1935 her novel *National Velvet* became a tremendous success both in England and in the United States with the movie version to follow and then a television series. Of her financial rewards Bagnold says ruefully that she made a great deal of money, perhaps more than twenty thousand pounds, from the first publication of *National Velvet* in America and in England but that eventually she lost it.

The problem was with taxes. Even though she had received a notice from Washington mentioning taxes, someone had told her that the memo would apply only to Americans. In the meantime she had bought an expensive gold cigarette case for Roderick, a pony for Laurian, and several typewriters. Three years later the tax warning was much stronger and the penalties had mounted. Not only that, she says, but her own investments had dropped, the pony had died, and the typewriters eventually wore out. To make matters worse, the radio and television rights had been included with the film so there was no further income from a radio version in America, England, and France. The result was that she paid in taxes all that she earned plus two thousand pounds borrowed from Roderick.

An interesting comment about the success of *National Velvet* is found in a letter of Evelyn Waugh from Beverly Hills (1947) to a friend in England. He had been in California as a guest of MGM to discuss making a film of *Brideshead Revisited*. He writes: "I am entirely obsessed with Forest Lawns & plan a long short story about it. I go there two or three times a week, am on easy terms with the chief embalmer . . . Did you know that the cadaver was referred to as 'the loved one' at F. L. I have seen dozens of loved ones half painted before the bereaved family saw them. In the Church of the Recessional at F. L. they have Enid Jones *National Velvet* in a glass case with a notice saying that it is comparable to *Alice in Wonderland* & was inspired by Rottingdean Church from which the Church of Recessional derives. . . ."[3]

In another letter, this to Nancy Mitford in August 1948, Evelyn Waugh says about Bagnold: "Lady Lampton was a Miss Jones but no relation to pen pusher (Enid). I used to despise p. p. until I went to the Church of the Recessional, Forest Lawn (Whispering Glades) and found that she was queen of the place with a special shrine in the reliquarium. So now I respect her but don't like her.[4]

Nancy Mitford had, apparently, called her "a sort of fearfully nice gym mistress."[5]

In 1938 Enid Bagnold had written the novel *The Squire* about a woman very much like herself, with four children, experiencing the birth of her fifth child. She remained faithful to her writing hours despite the greater demand for family involvement and a steady flow of visitors.

The visitors at Rottingdean were more difficult than the London visitors because they stayed longer. Roderick Jones had known General Smuts from his youth in South Africa and loved him; Enid thought him a showy hypocrite; however, they saw him many times over the years, and he became Timothy's godfather. Another friend of Roderick's from his South African days was Rudyard Kipling who had lived in Rottingdean for years. He was Laurian's godfather. Bagnold had always admired him and therefore was sympathetic in regard to the difficulty of Kipling's later years. He had achieved success too early, and the second part of his life was plagued by the ghost of that earlier triumph. Now he was lonely, seemingly cut off from life.

One of their dear friends and a constant visitor was Albrecht Bernstorff, counselor at the German Embassy (a prototype of Alberti in *The Loved and Envied*). Desmond MacCarthy and Prince Antoine were also regular visitors as were Vita Sackville-West and Harold Nicholson.

Among her guests and friends there was much talk about the world situation and in 1933 Bagnold felt compelled to go for a visit to Germany to see for herself what was happening. She took the car (sent ahead by ship to Hamburg) and drove about from village to village for ten days. Back in England, she wrote an article for the *Times,* which many of the politically aware considered "naive." The reactions surprised her. She was attacked, but not all of the mail was negative. Some people (including Rebecca West whom she respected greatly) confronted her at parties, and it was difficult to answer their questions. As she explained, she felt compelled to make the trip to Germany.

Albrecht Bernstorff was recalled in July 1933 and was succeeded as Counselor of Embassy by Prince Otto von Bismarck. The Joneses gave a farewell luncheon for Albrecht at which H. G. Wells and Harold Nicholson made good-bye speeches. He came back to England several times, but his open defiance of the Hitler movement eventually cost him his life. Because of Bagnold's article, she says, Hitler invited Roderick Jones to one of his rallies; he did not go, but when Ribbentrop came to London, he visited her, and she asked her husband for permission to invite him to lunch. He assented but suggested that she include someone who could "tackle" Ribbentrop. Austen Chamberlain and George Bernard Shaw accepted her invitation and, as she remembers, "out-flanked and out-talked" Ribbentrop.

When the war came, the composition of the household changed. Of the staff, the men joined the military forces, and the women went to work in the defense plants; and the Joneses moved temporarily across the way to a smaller house. A big blow to the family came when Timothy was seriously wounded in the war and lost a leg. In 1941 Jones resigned from Reuters, thereafter living a much simpler, more rustic life.

The Playwright

Enid Bagnold over the years had become increasingly fascinated by the theater. This interest may have been due to Desmond MacCarthy's influence. In 1943 her play *Lottie Dundass* was produced at the Vaudeville Theatre, starring Dame Sibyl Thorndike and Ann Todd; it ran for five months. In 1946 she wrote the play *Poor Judas* which later won the Arts Theatre Prize. Her last novel *The Loved and Envied* was published in 1951.

In 1952 she wrote the play *Gertie,* renamed *Little Idiot* in the London production. Herman Shumlin wanted to produce it in America with Glynis Johns in the lead, and Bagnold was persuaded to fly to New York for the rehearsals. *Gertie,* however, opened on a Wednesday and closed on Saturday; at the farewell party she met Irene Mayer Selznick, who later worked with her on the production of her next play *The Chalk Garden. The Chalk Garden* took several years in preparation but emerged a triumph, first in New York (1955) on her sixty-sixth birthday and then in London in 1956. For this play she received the Award of Merit for Drama from the American Academy of Arts and Letters in addition to prize money of one thousand dollars.

In the summer of 1958 she became good friends with Charles Laughton. He came often to visit, and she began to write a play for him but never finished it. Laughton's friendship serves as an interesting, if remote, connection between Bagnold and Bertolt Brecht. During his exile years in America Brecht had worked with Laughton on several plays, notably *Galileo* in which Charles Laughton had starred. There are, in addition to being friends with the famous actor, several points of similarity between Bagnold and Brecht. Like Bagnold, Brecht although nine years younger, had worked in an army hospital during World War I. He had been drafted as a medical orderly in 1918 in Augsburg. He, too, was fascinated by the French writers Villon, Rimbaud, and Verlaine, and as Bagnold had been, he was appreciative of Kipling's stories and ballads. In fact, the manly heroes of the ballads are said to serve as models for several of the characters in his plays.

During this period Bagnold had been working on a play that remained in the writing state for six years. She called it first *At the Top of His Form* and then changed the name to *The Last Joke.* It had been suggested to her by the suicide of Antoine's brother Emmanuel. John Gielgud was engaged for one of the leads, and then Ralph Richardson became interested in the play and wanted to be in it, but was miscast for the role he wished; this technicality was overlooked, but the problems that developed with both actors could not be. The final play was not like the original script, and she was unhappy with it; so, apparently, was everyone else.

Undaunted, Bagnold began work on *The Chinese Prime Minister.* She sent the first version to her agent in New York. In the meantime there was a great change in her life, for Roderick, who had been ill for some time, died. They had been married for forty-two years, and the adjustment was enormous. From now on, however, she tried to simplify life and to reduce her responsibilities.

Her agent loved the play, but again problems developed when the director wanted to make changes; nevertheless, a certain amount of rewriting began. With the hope, no doubt, that they might be engaged for the leads, Bagnold went to visit Lynn Fontanne and Alfred Lunt in Wisconsin. The leading lady was an actress of seventy, and Fontanne would have been perfect as would Lunt in the role of the globe-trotting husband. There was no persuading the two famous performers to leave their retirement; however, a friendship began that continued over the years, with Bagnold making regular visits to their home. Margaret Leighton finally played the part when *The Chinese Prime Minister* opened successfully in New York in January 1964.

Dame Edith Evans agreed to play the leading role in London if Bagnold would make more changes; she did. She attended the London opening (May 1965) with Terence Rattigan and T. C. Worsley. The effect of the play was not the same as it had been in New York, for Dame Edith played the role with too much sentiment, thereby, according to Bagnold, losing much of the meaning.

Instead of giving in to depression, she began work on another play. Within two years (1967) she had finished *Call Me Jacky;* this production fared even worse. As she said, "The critics loathed it at Guildford, loathed it in Brighton, and doubled the loathing at Oxford" (A, 357).

In 1976 a revised version of the play called *A Matter of Gravity* opened in New York with Katharine Hepburn in the lead. The critics praised Hepburn but cared little for the play. This was the last of the plays. Bagnold was disappointed that success in the theater had been so elusive, for she had wanted desperately to succeed.

Comments on the *Autobiography* and an Overview

In 1969 she published her *Autobiography.* Family and friends had for years urged her to record the unusual events of her life and to talk about the illustrious people she had known.

What strikes the reader is the tremendous vitality Enid Bagnold shows. She appears to be twenty-five instead of seventy-nine (eighty when it was published). She has a knack for dialogue but uses a clipped, impressionistic style often with little or no detail. Dates also seem unimportant to her, and she feels no particular need to follow chronological order when it suits her to move into the past or to cross into future events; the *Autobiography* is composed of a collection of delightful tales with some notable omissions. There is little information about their children and family life when the children were involvd with gymkhanas or their lives as teenagers and adults, not that these details are necessary to the value of the book. The story is about Enid Bagnold, after all. We see a version of the children, of course, in *National Velvet* and *The Squire*.

She never considered herself an intellectual and admitted being more uncomfortable with them than with the fun-loving social set with whom she chose later to spend most of her time. She was a product of her immediate past in that her reading preferences include writers of a more traditional literature: Rudyard Kipling, Arnold Bennett, and later, H. G. Wells, but she was also the product of the exciting spirit of the Impressionists and impressionistic literature. The need to find an artistic form for emotional truth was a great part of this movement. It seemed a spontaneous occurrence that so many writers began almost simultaneously to use what we now term impressionistic or stream-of-consciousness form: James Joyce, Marcel Proust, and Dorothy Richardson were the most notable examples at the time, but others then, including Katherine Mansfield (in the beginning) and Virginia Woolf, were there too. Bagnold says in the *Autobiography* that her friend Antoine (an acquaintance of Proust) influenced her writing and reading; the impressionistic style of much of her writing, therefore, comes as no surprise, but each of her books, heavily influenced by events in her life, is at the same time quite different in subject matter, background, and style from the others. She shows an individuality and a confidence that allows her to choose the literary form to suit her particular needs. In that way her work is unique. The challenge for form is equally strong when she abandons the novel and becomes the playwright.

She had always had a love for words. The diction in the novels is distinctive, the poet's ear and eye discernible, and this fascination with words is evident also in the sparkling dialogue of the plays, a dialogue which has become a trademark of her style. One sees here the influence of Oscar Wilde and of George Bernard Shaw, especially in the use of aphorisms, in the wit and humor, and in the vigorous spirit of her characters. Her plays show a whimsicality that hints of James Barrie's plays but in a more modern, a harsher environment. Her favorite modern playwright, she said, was Harold Pinter. One can see an affinity in the hint of mysticism, the unexplained ambiguous behavior of certain characters, sometimes not oriented to their surroundings, but a chief difference is that her characters are more verbal, and her people are definitely upper-class. She admired Edward Albee also, especially his *Who's Afraid of Virginia Woolf?*

Aside from the novel *National Velvet,* Enid Bagnold is associated in the minds of readers and theatergoers with drama and the stage, and she has earned a solid reputation as a modern playwright.

In Bagnold and her feminine contemporaries in the first quarter of the century, one notes an independence and a sexual emancipation that would have shocked the Victorians. They married late also. Dorothy Richardson was forty-four when she married; Rebecca West was thirty-eight; Virginia Woolf, thirty; Katherine Mansfield's first "real" marriage came at the age of thirty, and Enid Bagnold, too, married at thirty.

Her long life span allowed her to experience significant changes in the literary styles of her contemporaries from the early days of the century through the beginning of the 1980s. Enid Bagnold died on the last day of March 1981.

Chapter Two
The Early Works: A World at War

A Diary without Dates (1918)

In August 1914 when World War I began, Enid Bagnold was vacationing with her mother, father, and nineteen-year-old brother in Princetown on Dartmoor at the Duchy Hotel. She recalls the local excitement with the Dartmoor Prison gates opening and many of the warders marching out to join the army. The local populace was running alongside, accompanied by a band.

The women that could became volunteers, many training to become nurses' aides and receiving V.A.D. certificates for full-time hospital work. In Woolwich everyone rushed to the Royal Herbert Hospital at the bottom of Suter's Hill; for Enid it was a three-mile walk from home.

The hospital was staffed with nurses of an older order, a much tougher group than the newly trained women who had replaced them by war's end and who were more sympathetic and dedicated to service. The "old-time Sisters," as Enid says, "inherited from peace the idea that men in bed were malingerers" (*A,* 169). The older nurses looked impressive but did not gain the respect of the V.A.D.'s.

The *Diary* is an account of her experiences during two years of service at the Royal Herbert. Both books discussed in this chapter, *A Diary*—a true account—and *The Happy Foreigner*—a fictionalized account of her driving days in France, are written in impressionistic style. The result is that the truth of the one and the fiction of the other seem closely related. *A Diary* is indeed without dates; identifying marks are noticeably absent.

The book, however, has survived its time. An American edition was published in 1935, perhaps to share in the popularity of her novel *National Velvet,* and a paperback edition appeared in England in 1978. At its 1935 debut a *New York Times* reviewer praising the book

says: "After two decades and a plethora of war literature 'A Diary
Without Dates' is still worth reading and reprinting. Entirely unpre-
tentious, it communicates emotion directly and poignantly; it makes
one share the impact of war and suffering upon a youthful, intelligent, and very receptive mind.[1] At the same time, a reviewer for the
Christian Science Monitor praises her writing ability: "This book shows
the promise of an unusual power of writing."[2]

A Diary is divided into three sections: "Outside the Glass Doors,"
"Inside the Glass Doors," and "The Boys." Each part represents a
gradation of the author's increased experience and training. In the
first days of her apprenticeship she has limited contact with the patients but helps in the serving of meals, laying out the trays and silver and then bringing them to the wards. In the second part her work
takes her within the glass doors of the officers' wards, and in the last
section one sees her in yet a different world, that of the "common
men" whom the nurses call "The Boys."

As her apprenticeship days begin, she finds satisfaction in the discipline and in being part of an institution along with an admiration for
the nurses in their uniforms. The disillusioning elements and frustrations come later.

There is a purposeful distance between the officers and the
V.A.D.'s. One officer, however, seeks her out—a Mr. Pettitt. She
enjoys being admired from afar, but the relationship remains unre-
solved, and one never learns anything about him.

She soon discovers the insecurity of life here and the impermanence
of the hospital stay. Men are moved on quickly to the next stage, the
convalescent homes. She begins to sense the loneliness and knows
that, like nuns, nurses and patients will find no nearer friend than
God, but she becomes critical also of God who seems to be fickle in
his treatment of man: "Bolts, in the shape of sudden, whimsical orders are flung by an Almighty whom one does not see."[3]

She remarks on the manner in which patients come and go. A man
comes in on a stretcher, covered with a blanket; in death he leaves,
covered by a flag. It is always a shock to her that when a man dies,
his mattress is taken away to be disinfected, and no attempt is made
to keep his visiting parents from seeing the bare coils of the bed. The
callousness of this attitude dismays her.

On one visit to the wards she is shaken to see three red screens
around the bed of the person about whom she is to inquire. As she
waits, one screen is removed: "The man I was to inquire for has no
nostrils; they were blown away, and he breathes through two pieces

of red rubber tubing: it gave a more horrible look to his face than I have ever seen. The Sister came out and told me she thought he was 'not up to much.' I think she means he is dying." (*DD*, 8). He had been nearly well before developing pneumonia and had begun following the hospital routine even to coming to take tea.

Even though there is a joy in belonging to the hospital, there is also a joy in leaving it. When she goes in the evening, she prepares for the climb up the hill, to home. Most often this is a pleasant ritual. There are no details about her outside life once she leaves the hospital.

Years later, at sixty-nine, reviewing the past, Bagnold could in her *Autobiography* compare the two wars and speak of those early days at the hospital.

She was sent down with a group to meet the trains coming in with the wounded. The soldiers came directly from the battlefields with their bloody bandages. Among the trainloads was one of badly wounded German soldiers. These prisoners were afraid to accept even the tea offered them for they had been warned that the English would poison them. One was closer to the suffering in the first world war, she maintains. In the second world war there were no trains of the wounded.

When Bagnold graduates to the area inside the glass doors, she discovers that ward life is hectic, and she becomes increasingly critical of the sisters for their misplaced sense of values. They seem more anxious to impress visitors than to take care of their patients. Even the plants in the ward are arranged on a table by the door for the benefit of guests.

At Christmas time, along with her many duties, she is in charge of putting up the decorations in the ward. The men have hung up their stockings on walking sticks over the ends of beds, and from under mattresses. She is also engrossed in errands, washing, bed-making. Mr. Pettitt reappears briefly, but she is not encouraging, apparently refusing a lunch invitation. She says, "When a woman says she cannot come to lunch it is because she doesn't want to. Let this serve as an axiom for every lover. A woman who refuses lunch refuses everything" (*DD*, 45). One can see already her fondness for aphorisms, which appear plentifully in her later work, especially in the plays.

It is difficult to imagine—in our more modern hospitals—conditions that she mentions without intentionally singling them out. For example, the cold weather is a problem. She says, "There was a long

silence in the ward to-night. It was so cold that no one spoke. It is
a gloomy ward. . . . The fire smokes dreadfully. The patients sat
round the fire with their 'British warms' over their dressing gowns
and the collars turned up" (*DD*, 67). Earlier she described the coming in of the fog: "The fog developed all day yesterday, piling up
white and motionless against the window panes. . . . By seven
o'clock even the long corridor was as dim as the alley outside. No one
thought of shutting the windows—I doubt whether they will
shut . . . and the fog rolled over the sill in banks and round the open
glass doors, till even the white cap of a Sister could hardly be seen as
she passed" (*DD*, 38–39).

When a new convoy comes in with the wounded, there is excitement for the first time in the ward, and she sees the further step, the
soldiers becoming the patients. It is time then to "wash and fetch and
carry" (*DD*, 73).

She becomes more aware now of the personalities on the ward, add-
ing occasional touches of humor as with Captain Thomson, who is
described as tall and dark, with soft eyes. When he leaves, he gives
her his business card, offering to sell to the nurses crepe de chine
wholesale. He, it turns out, is an underwear salesman.

It is frustrating, however, to receive no definite picture of the man
in bed #11 with whom she has temporarily fallen in love; she is not
allowed to show partiality or personal interest in any patient. When
she does, she finds the other patients and the sisters on the ward her
enemies. She relates, "I am alive, delirious, but not happy. I am at
anyone's mercy; I have lost thirty friends in a day. The thirty-first is
in bed No. 11" (*DD*, 79). There is no real contact, no interchange
of confidences between the two, and for the reader, unhappily, no further information.

One day she comes on duty and finds an empty bed. Number 11
has been quickly and quietly transferred to another hospital. She realizes that she will never see him again. Later she asks the sister in
charge how permanently she is in disgrace. The nurse answers, "Not
at all . . . now" (*DD*, 84).

In the final section, "The Boys," Bagnold steps down, as she says,
"from chintz covers and lemonade to the main army and lemon-water
(*DD*, 97). On their ward, for instance, instead of squeezing twenty-
six lemons twice a day as for the officers' lemonade, she now squeezes
two lemons into an old jug and "hopes for the best about the sugar"
(*DD*, 97). She is shyer here in the "Tommies" ward, and she doesn't

think of the men as "boys," as the sisters do. She feels that they do not treat the men with dignity. In fact, one of the things that upsets her most is the attitude toward the "Tommies."

Individual incidents are frustrating, as with Smiff, a soldier nine months in the hospital. She complains, "His foot is off, and to-night for the first time the doctor had promised that he should be wheeled into the corridor. But it was forgotten, and I am too new to jog the memory of the gods" (*DD*, 97–98). She is not allowed to remind the doctor.

She speaks of the pain that is obvious in the men's faces but that often the nurses do not seem to understand or have become insensitive to. She says, "The pain of one creature cannot continue to have a meaning for another. It is almost impossible to nurse a man well whose pain you do not imagine. A deadlock" (*DD*, 101)! The two conditions exist and yet must be reconciled. At an unknown point the pain seems to become more bearable. She relates the example of Rees who wakes up sobbing: " 'Don' go away, nurse . . .' He holds my hand in a fierce clutch, then releases it to point in the air, crying, 'There's the pain!' as though the pain filled the air and rose to the rafters. As he wakes it centralizes, until at last comes the moment when he says, 'Me arm aches cruel,' and points to it. Then one can leave him" (*DD*, 102).

There is Gayner of the Expeditionary Forces, whose wounds have caused him to make the rounds of the hospitals. He will not read, write, or even speak to his neighbor and is attentive only when his wounds are being dressed: "If one asks him something of the history of his wound his tone holds such a volume of bitterness and exasperation that one feels that at any moment the locks of his spirit might cease to hold" (*DD*, 109). Later, Gayner suffers from hysteria. He believes he is getting tetanus. He complains that his jaws want to close and that he can't keep them open. She wonders how many men he has seen die of tetanus, but even after the doctor diagnoses his condition as hysteria, no one reassures him that he does not have tetanus. The V.A.D.'s are not allowed to pass on such information.

Most of the soldiers feel that their lives have been suspended, and they have no plans for the future. Some adjust more quickly to their difficult circumstances. Scutts has eleven wounds with two crippled arms, but he does not view his life as stopped; he watches for the mail, eagerly waiting for his new eye. He has plans for a six months' holiday and perhaps a walking tour through Britain.

Among the duties in this ward when time permits is the sewing of sandbags and the making of splints, which Bagnold considers gentle work and which allows time to look and listen more carefully to patients in the ward. From the hospital they can hear the guns: "Those distant guns again to-night . . . Now a lull and now a bombardment; again a lull, and then batter, batter, and the windows tremble. Is the lull when they go over the top? I can only think of death to-night. I tried to think just now, 'What is it, after all! Death comes anyway; this only hastens it.' But that won't do; no philosophy helps the pain of death. It is pity, pity, pity, that I feel, and sometimes a sort of shame that I am here to write at all" (DD, 103–4).

One learns that another attack has begun; one convoy arrives at night and another in the morning. She speaks of the stages of adjustment of these new men. At first they are simply happy to be alive; then, in a few days, they realize that they might be better, and in a few weeks they are more critical and wonder if indeed this is happiness. Birthdays may be important, but the most important anniversary for all dates from the time they were wounded. "One and all, they know the exact hour and minute on which their bit of metal turned them home" (DD, 139).

The diary entries are not separated by days; the impressions merge so that one has little idea of passing time. Neither are there transitions between the incidents or thoughts.

The persona in *A Diary without Dates,* in this case Enid Bagnold herself, reminds one of Dorothy Richardson's Miriam of the *Pilgrimage* novels, especially in the aloofness and slight touch of superiority with which she manages her life. The *Diary*'s impressionism is akin to the style of the Richardson works which, though classified as fiction, are essentially autobiographical. A significant difference between the two writers, though they both show sensitivity, is that Bagnold has a sense of humor. She shows also a greater enthusiasm for life.

When Virago Press issued the paperback version of the book in 1978 in Britain, reviewer David Mitchell in the *Times Literary Supplement* acknowledged that many of the most poignant impressions of the time came from the pages of the diaries of the tens of thousands of auxiliary nurses and orderlies. "*A Diary Without Dates,*" he says, "recreates with notable economy the atmosphere of the hospital. . . . Artfully constructed around a scaffolding of gnomic reflections, the book has some affinity with Logan Pearsall Smith's Trivia, published in the same year (1918). 'Pity is exhaustible. What a terrible discovery!' . . . Publication of *A Diary* enraged authorities. Yet the book, though penetrating, is not malicious or resentful. . . . The pervading philosophy resembles that of Mabel Dearmer, who, from a field hospital in Serbia, wrote to her sons: 'It is all ignorance and folly and we are working out through it to ordinary sense. The only way to see war is from a hospital.' "[4]

Despite the hospital experience, or because of it, Enid Bagnold was eager to become involved again in (civilian) war activities; thus, shortly thereafter, at the cessation of hostilities, she volunteered her services as a driver in France.

The Happy Foreigner (1920)

Bagnold seems to have had a fascination for motor cars from the early days of the first family automobile. In 1902 and 1903, she recalls, everyone ran down to the main road to see a car coming. Sometime around 1904 her father bought a Cadillac, and with much excitement she and her mother drove about the countryside with him.

She became acquainted also with the technical and mechanical aspects of the car. It became almost a family project. On Sunday afternoons they polished the brass of the radiator, the horn, and the lamps. Her father built an electrically lit pit for the car so that its interior works were readily accessible.

Bagnold's experience with her family's car proved valuable, for the Englishwomen who volunteered as drivers for the French army during the last months of the war and immediately after the armistice, were responsible for the cars assigned to them. At night the automobiles were kept at a shifting home base in a common garage, but the assigned trips, driving for French officers, often kept them out for several days at a time. During most of her stay in France Bagnold's car was a Rochet and later a big shiny Renault of which she was proud. These experiences were the basis for her first novel, *The Happy Foreigner*. In the story the central character is Fanny, a young Englishwoman through whose eyes the reader views this war-torn countryside.

Many of the Americans who volunteered their services in France and Italy during World War I served as ambulance drivers; among them were writers such as Ernest Hemingway, John Dos Passos, and E. E. Cummings, but there were few women drivers. In *The Happy Foreigner* Fanny mentions that the Russians and the French found it hard to understand how the English could allow their women to mingle so freely with men as the drivers obviously had to do. The Englishwomen received no pay, only room and board.

The book is arranged in four parts: each deals with a section of the country to which Fanny is assigned in her driving duties with the French army. Places are important in this book and carefully detailed, sometimes in an almost objective fashion. Few comments deal with the varying degrees of destruction and waste and now and then beauty in the landscape. All is noted and accepted, often with wonder, occasionally with dismay, but Fanny is never sorry for herself nor does she bemoan her situation. She shows an amazing degree of control, maturity, courage, and stoicism in dealing with the conditions in which she finds herself.

The love story is a major element of the novel, and yet it is treated so lightly in impressionistic style that we learn almost nothing about Julien or the details of their encounters. As to Fanny, we have no indication of why she is here—how she came to this point, what her past life and family are. We know only that she is English, and that her father is an English officer. Still, the novel works and the magic is there, even if the reader has no sense of the characters' backgrounds. They appear as full-blown, believable people, if rootless. It is as though we are allowed to view this one section of their lives unconnected with past or future. Through Fanny's mind we share this experience which is focused on her immediate surroundings and her love for Julien.

The same sparcity of material governs Fanny's English friend Stewart, also a lady volunteer driver. It is Stewart in Metz who defends the credibility of the women drivers by passing the test, being able to operate the Rochet. All of the volunteers, apparently, are from good families.

In addition to place, time is important since the areas visited are the battlefields almost immediately after the cessation of fighting: towns are destroyed; enemy equipment lies where it was deserted; Russian prisoners of war are still present in camps as taken by the Germans, and no one seems to know what to do with them; people have been displaced; the natives gradually come back to see what is retrievable and slowly begin to rebuild. There are footloose Americans everywhere who want nothing more than to be sent home. The Americans, however, have food and supplies, while food in the French camps is scarce. Other ethnic groups wandering about the countryside include Annamites (Vietnamese) and Chinese.

When Fanny first arrives at Bar le Duc amidst the rain and the mud, it is November 1918. Several of the eight Englishwomen have already been there for some months. They are assigned whatever cars from a fleet of thirty are available, and now and then an ambulance. Their living quarters consist of a tarred hut of wood and tarpaulin divided into eight cubicles with walls of gray paper; a small sitting room is at one end of the building. The descriptions here are exact, carefully selected, most of them dealing with place, as in the following:

Outside the black hut the jet-black night poured water down. Inside, the eight cubicles held each a woman, a bed and a hurricane lantern. Fanny, in her paper box, listened to the scratching of a pen next door, then turned her eyes as a new and nearer scratching caught her ear. A bright-eyed rat stared at her through the hole it had made in the wall.

"Food is in!"

Out of the boxes came the eight women to eat pieces of dark meat from a tin set on the top of the sittingroom stove—then cheese and bread. The watery night turned into sleet and rattled like tin-foil on the panes.[5]

Fanny does not complain or elaborate on difficulties. She says, "Those who had to be out early had left before the daylight, still with their lanterns swinging in their hands; had battled with the cold cars in the unlighted garage, and were moving alone across the long desert of the battlefields" (*HF,* 8). She passed the test on her first morning with an old ambulance. On the second morning she was assigned a Charron and began her first run.

The weeks go by, and Fanny feels a great loneliness, yet is glad to have come. There is plenty of work to keep the women busy. They drive officers to the various villages on rounds of two hundred kilometers a day. Mayors of ruined villages present claims for damage caused by French troops stationed there. The officers must inspect motor parks. Also, they search through purchases of old iron to identify thefts from the battlefields.

Then suddenly the whole group is transferred to Metz in the Lorraine area where quite different living quarters and something of a social life are offered since Marechal Petain is there, and the commandant wishes to make the town appear prosperous and lively to prove to the inhabitants that they will be better off with the French than under the Germans. The Englishwomen are recruited in their off-hours as dancing partners at the local military functions. It is here that Fanny meets her young French captain, the commandant's aid, Julien Chatel.

But when the Englishwomen first arrive at the garage area, their suitability is questioned. The brigadier assigns the cars: four Rochets, two Delages, two Fiats. The male drivers, working on their cars, are ready to mock them. Are the Rochets too heavy for the women to handle? When it is suggested, the test comes. Stewart, the only other young woman described, insists on being allowed to try. The cranking and the starting of the car are the obstacles. Now the honor of all is at stake:

Stewart, seizing the handle, could not turn it. In the false night of the shed the lights shone on polished lamps, on glass and brass, on French eyes which said: "That's what comes of it!"—which were ready to say—"March out again, Englishwomen, ridiculous and eager and defeated!"

Fanny, looking neither to right nor left, prayed under her breath—"Stewart, Stewart, we can never live in this shed if you can't start her. And if you can't, nobody else can. . . ." (*HF*, 31)

She does start it, and the trial is over; the women are accepted. Fanny has just met Julien, and they have had their first meeting at the cathedral. The attraction was instantaneous, but both are hesitant to admit their interest, and as they part, Fanny is afraid that she will not see him again.

At this crucial time she is assigned to drive a Russian colonel to Verdun, eighty miles away. The colonel is shocked to find a woman driver assigned to him and believes, one discovers later, that this is the commandant's method of dispatching him and that he will not arrive at his destination. The lieutenant riding with them is the one who apprises Fanny of the Russian's reactions as they proceed. The trip to Verdun, the garrison town in eastern France, is one of the highlights of the book.

The siege of Verdun, one of the major engagements of World War I, was apparently the bloodiest single military operation. In spite of continuing German attacks, the French forces under Generals Petain and Nivelle held out. During the campaign over a million men, French and German, battled over the Verdun territory. Now there was desolation. Fanny views the countryside: "They touched the brink of the battlefields. . . . The road grew wilder and wilder and took on the air of a burnt-out moor, mile after mile of grey, stricken grass, old iron, and large upturned stones. Wherever a pair of blasted trees was left at the road's side a notice hung in the mid-air, on wires slung from tree to tree across the road. 'Halt—Autos!' shouted the square black German orders from the boards which swung and creaked in the wind. . . " (*HF*, 46).

Interestingly enough, the objects in the landscape, even in its present desolation, reflect the former violence: "stricken grass," "blasted trees," "road. . . wilder and wilder," "upturned stones." The effective description of the abandoned territory continues: "For miles and miles nothing living was to be seen, neither animal, nor motor, nor living man; only the stray fires of the Chinese fluttered here and there like blue and red marshfires a mile or so back from the main road. . ." (*HF*, 46). At last they pass into the suburbs of the city: "Verdun stood upright as by a miracle, a coarse lace of masonry—not one house was whole" (*HF*, 47).

Soldiers are clearing the streets; the civilians have not yet returned. In answer to Fanny's question as to where people sleep, she is told that they sleep *beneath* Verdun; there are fifteen kilometers of tunnel underground. They locate the special entrance into the hill with the gateway, defended by barbed wire and guns.

At this point Fanny discovers that she will not be driving back to Metz. "You are lent to us for five days. They should have told you!" the lieutenant tells her (*HF*, 49). Having brought no provisions or extra clothes, Fanny nevertheless accepts the situation. The tunnels branch out and lead them to an area of sleeping accommodations for visiting officers. She is curious and surprised to find the thriving network of activity; twenty roofless cubicles of light wood line the stone wall, each raised slightly above the damp floor. These are rooms assigned to visiting officers, whose duty requires their spending a night in Verdun.

Later, Fanny walks through the busy corridors and realizes suddenly that she is being stared at. Seventy or eighty officers, eating dinner at a long trestle table, are astonished to find a woman in their midst.

The daytime driving in the area consists of a tour of inspection for the Red Cross. The Russian colonel is in the process of visiting the camps of the Russian prisoners liberated from Germany. Fanny goes out into Verdun at night to check the car and prepare it for the following day. She realizes her limitations: "She set to work on her car which stood in the shelter of an archway opposite, and for half an hour the sky trembled unregarded above her head. When she had finished she stood back and gazed at the Rochet with an anxious friendly enmity—the friendship of an infant with a lion. 'The garage is eighty miles away,' she sighed, 'with its friendly men who know all where I know so little. . . Ah, do I know enough? What have I left undone?' For she felt, what was the truth, that the whole expedition depended on her, that the stately Russian had perhaps never known what it was to have a breakdown. . . " (*HF,* 55).

Fanny forms definite impressions of the American and the French soldiers that she meets along the way. She finds that the French are very poor and usually tenderhearted and that the Americans behave like children. Yet they have reputations for brutality and are placed as guards over the Russian prisoners for that reason. The prisoners cannot be freed until the logistics of the evacuation can be carried out.

Back in Metz, Fanny resumes her friendship with Julien. She splurges and orders a dress made for a costume ball. On the day before the big event she receives a possible two-day driving assignment to Germany; her disappointment is great, and there is much suspense until she returns in time to help with the last-moment finishing of the dress and dances through a blissful evening.

Breakdowns do occur, and Fanny finds herself stranded on one run, with a broken rear axle. Her "client" has received a ride from a passing truck, having promised to telephone her garage, while she remains with the car. She waits from morning until daylight recedes, and the weather becomes bitter cold. Night approaches, and, alone with her flashlight, she sees several dark figures that have come to raid her food supply. They snatch the food and run, but she is severely shaken, expecting an attack. By the beam of her flashlight she catches a glimpse of the retreating Chinese figures who disappear into the darkness but otherwise offer no further harm. Julien arrives then with a lieutenant to rescue her, having received word from the garage late in the day. The lieutenant remains with the car as Fanny and Julien return to town.

The corps of drivers moves again, this time to Precy, a village on the Oise River. This section of the book is entitled, "The Forests of Chantilly." Julien is in a village close by, and the idyllic love affair becomes most intense at this point; yet the reader sees very little of it. Finally, Julien is instrumental in having the group sent to Charle-ville where he has land and a former factory. He has received word that within days he will be back in Paris and in civilian life; he prom-ises that he will visit Fanny in Charleville at least once a week.

Parting is painful, but they both accept the necessity of it and the possible estrangement that the future may bring. Julien has told Fanny about a woman in his life, but one never knows what the rela-tionship between them is—fiancée? Wife? Aside from knowing that Julien is concerned about his factory and is, no doubt, wealthy, no further information is given; he remains a mystery.

When they report to Charleville, Fanny manages to be assigned an abandoned house to herself. She is hoping for visits from Julien, visits which never materialize. Several weeks later, on the day before she is to return to England, he appears and asks her to drive him to the area several miles away where the factory and his former home are located. It is evening as she leaves him there, never telling him, although she had planned to, that she will be gone the next day. She has realized that the idyl is over; their lives are pointed in different directions, and she must now give up her fantasies.

Arthur Calder-Marshall makes an interesting comparison between the endings of *The Happy Foreigner* and *A Farewell to Arms,* both nov-els whose themes are "the passionate attempt to secure personal hap-piness escaping from the desolation of war and the trammels of military discipline." He maintains that Hemingway realized that the love affair could not endure beyond the end of the war and demobili-zation. As a sentimentalist, however, he could not accept the idea of true love as temporary: ". . . To create the illusion of permanence, Hemingway was forced to kill his heroine off. He gave the novel in consequence a heroic facade, an appearance of tragic strength which masked his weakness. Miss Bagnold is in fact far the tougher of the two. Though less violent, her conclusion is stronger, when Fanny and Julien stand together on the mountain looking down upon his civilian future, which despite its worthiness she recognises as separate from her own."[6]

This parting of the ways may be realistic, but Fanny has already experienced disillusion in the weeks of waiting for Julien to appear, and his coming now is, in her eyes, too late; the ache may remain, but the spell has been broken.

Considering the bittersweet ending, why did Enid Bagnold call her novel *The Happy Foreigner?* The title is, in one sense, ironic. There is irony in the fact that Fanny, the seemingly happy foreigner, is at the end sad, disappointed in the turn of events, concealing the ache that comes with the realization that the dream is over; and yet Fanny's nature is positive. She has not lost the "astonishment of living." The other characters see her as a survivor, confident. She knows this about herself and has the courage to face the truth. In that sense Fanny remains "happy," adjusted to life's conditions, stoically accepting what each day brings. She may not forget Julien, but one is sure that she will recover.

Chapter Three
Serena Blandish: or The Difficulty of Getting Married

Biographical Elements

The idea for *Serena Blandish* came ten years before the actual writing of the novel, in the pre-World War I and war years when Enid Bagnold was attending the parties of the Baroness d'Erlanger. At this time she met the young lady of seventeen who was to be the model for Serena, an extraordinary and beautiful girl. Bagnold had become friends with a charming lady who had invited her to her family home. Among her sisters was a silent, innocent-looking girl whom the others considered uncommunicative and secretive, out of touch with life.

The irony of this situation is revealed when the young sister one day telephones Bagnold to borrow one hundred pounds for an abortion. When Bagnold, quietly shocked, asks if the man won't help, the girl admits that she doesn't know who the father is. In fact, after Bagnold has supplied the money and the operation is past, she asks the young girl how many men she has slept with and finds that she has no idea. She admits further that she gets no pleasure from men but rather from being accommodating and saying yes; apparently by her very appearance at parties, though she says little, she is immediately surrounded by men.

In her *Autobiography* Bagnold also describes at some length the eccentric Baroness Catherine d'Erlanger, prototype of the Countess Flor di Folio in *Serena Blandish,* who takes Serena into her household as an amusing project. In the novel the countess is wayward, lively, autocratic, a woman of much worldly experience with little judgment and nothing to do but seek new pleasures. On the particular day when she picks up Serena, she has already acquired a menagerie which includes a caged peacock, a parrot, and a monkey. Serena sees herself as part of the collection, as the countess means that she should.

When the book was published, the indignant Baroness d'Erlanger banished Bagnold from her London home and threatened to sue. Bagnold had not realized, she says, that the invented character was so unflattering to the original or that the baroness would fail to see the humor of the spoof.

The Plot

The story goes as follows. Serena's family has become poor, and her mother tells Serena that she must work, train herself for a job, perhaps as an actress. Serena seeks among her many men friends enough money, only two pounds a week actually, for six months of training so that she can support herself; however, none of her ex-lovers is generous enough to donate a shilling. All give excuses, and she forgives them.

It occurs to her then that she should marry. At this point the countess meets her and invites her to come and live in her household for two months; there Serena will make a brilliant marriage. It is Serena's responsibility, however, to make the most of her charm and bring about this event, and the countess is quite certain that Serena will succeed. What the countess does not know is that Serena has a weakness. She cannot say no nor hold back her favors long enough to wait for a marriage proposal.

Serena does attract attention from the many guests in the household and at the dinner parties. Martin, the butler, becomes a confidant and tries, to a certain extent, to help her, but she has no success as to offers of marriage. One splendid opportunity with Lord Ivor Cream is lost when she agrees to meet him for tea in his apartment, and her ingrained habit of pleasing prompts her to go to bed with him. She has been warned that the giving of favors, especially the ultimate one, is strictly forbidden if one is to get a proposal of marriage.

As time goes on, Serena becomes more anxious and the countess more impatient. At last, just as the countess has given her an ultimatum, and she is to be evicted, the wealthy, mysterious Count Montague D'Costa proposes; he is an acquaintance of a princess who is also a guest of the countess. He and Serena can only gaze at each other in admiration, for he speaks almost no English. He falls in love with her and proposes marriage, although they have had no more contact than a few moments in public view and almost no private conversation.

A whirlwind of activity ensues, for the countess arranges the marriage as quickly as possible. The day before the wedding D'Costa's relatives arrive; Serena has not seen them, but suddenly she realizes that something is amiss. Everyone is upset, yet no one cares to inform her. She meets the relatives, seemingly Portuguese, and appreciates their joyful acceptance of her. Then that evening she meets the count's mother who has just arrived unexpectedly. With a shock, Serena sees that she is a full-blooded (Nicaraguan) Indian, and Martin informs her later that although the count is rich, his title is not bona fide. As the book ends, Serena, overwhelmed, goes through with the ceremony. At least she is married.

Style and Characterization

The technique and style of *Serena Blandish* are quite different from anything Enid Bagnold had written before or would write thereafter. Although the novel is contemporary in subject matter, the style is that of the eighteenth-century philosophical novel and Voltaire's *Candide* in particular. Like *Candide* it sparkles with wit, irony, and cynical pronouncements about life and people; and like many eighteenth-century novels, it has a subtitle expressing the theme.

The humor is often tongue-in-cheek and directed toward Serena, her ex-lovers, and the motley group assembled at the house of the countess. Serena is wily in one sense and yet naive and guileless, making grievous errors in judgment and apparently unaware of the hypocrisy, the greed, and the lack of compassion with which she is surrounded. There is humor in her self-assessment before she meets the countess, as she acknowledges her own beauty and the qualities that should make her suitable for marriage. She considers that she has not yet followed her heart and that when she dares do that in the security of marriage, she is confident that she will be constant. She sees herself as docile, beautiful, and young, and marriage as a difficult state to attain, for no one yet has urged marriage, despite all of her excellent qualities.

Because she has been discreet and secretive, her family, friends, and general acquaintances are unaware of her peccadilloes. She "seems" to be a virgin, and therefore, she reasons, for all practical purposes, she "is."

The beginning of the novel has much of the same fable quality as *Candide,* a quality which is extended also to the rest of the book. Enid

Bagnold begins the story with a description of Serena: "Among all the women who lived in a garden city adjoining the southern docks of London, none was so charming or so uncommon as Miss Serena Blandish, a young girl of nineteen to whom nature had given every grace of figure, face, ankle, wrist, and expression."[1]

Likewise, *Candide* begins with a description of the young hero, the pattern of which Bagnold seems to have had in mind: "There lived in Westphalia, in the castle of my Lord the Baron of Thunder-ten-tronckh, a young man on whom nature had bestowed the most agreeable manners. His face was the index to his mind. He had an upright heart, with an easy frankness; which, I believe, was the reason he got the name of Candide."[2]

Serena has the same traits, the same easy frankness and uprightness of heart. After a rebuke from a former friend, in response to a call for aid, she realizes that she did not understand his "private heart," and she comes to the conclusion that her own heart is kinder than those of the people she has met: "the truth is," she finally reflected, "that a woman will love anything, from a pekinese dog, a drunkard, a wife beater to such as he who writes this letter. I do not wish to flatter myself, but my true experience is that my own heart is the kindest I have yet met in the world" (119). The reader sees the pathos of the situation and sympathizes with Serena, yet is always conscious of the humor. Serena and Candide, however, are often victims since they are trusting and innocent of the machinations and heartlessness of their fellowman.

Of other likenesses between the two novels, Candide acquires a philosopher friend and confidant named Martin. He, like Martin, the butler confidant in *Serena,* is cynical but loyal.

Earlier Candide has hired a valet-companion named Cacambo who is one-quarter Spanish, and the son of a half-breed Argentinian mother (the count in *Serena* has a Spanish father and an Indian mother); Serena is befriended briefly by a member of the princess's entourage called Cuckoo. He, like Cacambo, has learned to live by his wits, and saves Serena from ruin when the jeweler comes to retrieve his diamond ring; Cacambo saves Candide's life in Paraguay when they are captured by the Indians.

Although the story lines of *Serena Blandish* and *Candide* differ, each has a poor protagonist seeking survival and perhaps fortune in a hostile world in which she/he experiences numerous rebuffs and losses before the final gain. The final gain, however, is ambiguous and

uncertain, a hollow victory. Candide is finally reunited with Cune-
gonde, his long-lost love, but now he finds that she is ugly and no
longer desirable. In the same way Serena finally achieves her goal: she
marries the count but discovers that he is not what he appears, rich
perhaps, but not a true count, the illegitimate son of an Indian
woman, and almost inarticulate in the English language.

Quests for Knowledge

In the vein of the protagonist of the philosophical novel Serena is
seeking knowledge: the major quest involves finding by what magic
a man may be brought to propose. A secondary quest is concerned
with finding what kind of woman it is who obtains diamonds. Most
of the novel is concerned with the first, how to obtain a proposal.

In the search direct inquiry has not been useful. Serena has asked
an ex-suitor by what behavior on his wife's part he was brought to
offer her all his life and half of his money. The humorous implication
here is that selfish man, putting a higher value on his money than his
life, will part with all of his life but only half of his money. The man
replies that although he is content with his life, he cannot imagine
or remember why he did it.

No one seems to have a satisfactory answer. The style of the novel
is reminiscent also of the eighteenth-century mock-heroic, the extrav-
agant show of the banal. In fact, in the banquet scene as Serena is
seated next to the count, with Martin trying to get her attention to
warn her not to forget herself, one is reminded of Pope's Sylph in
"The Rape of the Lock," trying to warn Belinda of impending danger
as she sits at the table. In neither case does the lady pay attention to
the signals.

In one scene, for the novel seems to fall naturally into major scenes,
Serena finds herself with a duke's daughter and a fashion model. In
their talk of marriage the duke's daughter, also afraid that she will
not marry, discusses the disadvantages of being nobility; part of this
is the necessity for a young man to provide an opulent life-style. She
has been engaged one week to a professional billiard player and is
fearful that he may break the engagement. She explains to Serena that
there are not many bachelors willing to take on the burden of marrying a duke's daughter. Keeping a stable of horses is less pompous and
more fun. Not only that, but dukes' daughters cannot marry above
themselves since there are few prospects. Marrying downward brings

a certain appeal to the commoner but also bewilderment and no plea-sure.

Serena finds, as do the characters in *Rasselas* and *Candide,* that things are not as they seem. What appears as happy on the surface is deceiving. There is much unhappiness underneath. The model, named Manila, also unmarried, has confessed that she has been on show from morning to night—dressed for success—but nothing she wears belongs to her.

The duke's daughter has remarked that humility seems no attribute for a young woman, to which Serena answers sadly: "As for me, hu-mility is the keynote of my character, I cannot uproot it. But I recog-nize at every fresh adventure its fatal effect upon my fortunes." The image, she says, affects her lovers so that instead of bowing before her beauty, they are aware instead of her vulnerability; she is prepared for abuse and thus receives it, and like terriers they "chase the flying cat solely because it flies." She has never demanded anything, she says, and consequently has never received anything (153–54).

Manila, on the other hand, is irritated by this exchange of confi-dences and, anxious to retrieve her pride, confronts her fashion-de-signer companion as he enters, telling him that she will no longer put up with all this nonsense. She is quitting her job and leaving. The designer is intrigued by this sudden rebellion and pursues his best model, not to rehire her but to propose marriage. Serena is amazed.

This theme of the difficulty of getting married is embodied in yet another character who craves marriage—to the count, in particular. She is his secretary, a tall Amazonlike lady swathed in soft feminine attire but with the voice of a male and a masculine-looking neck and muscles. She speaks to Serena of the disadvantages of being a woman and tried to commit suicide ten years before by jumping into the Seine. With a lack of beauty and strong dreams of marriage but with increasing frustration and full of rage and misery, she wanted to end her life. From the time of her rescue, she confesses, she has changed her life, shifted hopes, and all but changed her sex, resolved to have a male personality. But now that the secretary is in love, as Serena notes, she is trying to appear more feminine.

One of the sad but bizarre events, although little attention is given it, is her second and successful suicide attempt—this time in the Thames—during the bustle of arrangements for Serena's wedding to the count. Although the secretary (never given a name) has tried to discourage Serena from taking the count seriously, one realizes that perhaps he has some endearing qualities. The princess, too, although in her sixties, has previously tried to pursue him with no success. The count is given a spectacular buildup prior to his entrance, especially since the princess mistakenly speaks of him as a romantic figure, rich, hermitlike, of Portuguese royalty with oil holdings in America, a home in Paris, and estates in Argentina, so that when he does appear, Serena sees his interest in her as a miracle.

Along with the marriage quest is the inquiry as to how to acquire diamonds. Serena has determined to stand at the door of an exclusive jewelry shop to see what kind of woman obtains these expensive stones: "I will stand here a little and see what men and women go in at the door, what charm that I know nothing of, what beauty greater than mine, can procure for itself the diamond out of that promise." (86).

The jeweler sees her and invites her in, but she tells him she has no money. There is humor in her childlike honesty. He admires her beauty and then agrees with her theory that the first jewel is necessary to attract other jewels. He states in fact that he has never seen a man buying diamonds for a woman who does not already have them. "If you had but one ring men would add to it others; but to have nothing, to be penniless, is not to excite sympathy but disdain" (89). He offers to lend her a diamond ring for one month but changes this offer to two weeks when he discovers that she is looking for a husband rather than a bevy of admirers who might order their jewels from him.

A happy Serena leaves the store. Later, on a bus, she engages in conversation an attractive young man; a poet he calls himself. He has obligingly paid her bus fare, but before she realizes what is happening, he steals the ring and makes a hasty retreat. Thereafter, part of the suspense involves Serena's trying to elude the jeweler when he comes to retrieve his ring.

What has been learned from this pursuit of knowledge? Nothing, really. Serena has become increasingly cynical, but before final conclusions can be reached, the count appears, and, due to accident, Serena cannot speak encouragingly nor apply her usual behavior and therefore wins the proposal. Neither has she learned how to acquire diamonds, but with no further effort on her part she receives for the engagement an exquisite emerald ring. Again, she is mystified, not knowing why she has succeeded.

Use of Aphorisms and Philosophical Truths

As Voltaire does, Enid Bagnold makes use of aphorisms and gems of wisdom. For instance, Serena reflects on the relationship of men and women and decides that they treat each other in a very strange manner. She says, "The world is full of intimacy without friendship, love without service, admiration without a single wish that the object of it should be happy" (94–95).

There is in the statements much use of balance and parallelism.

In another instance she considers the subjects of money and affection. Money, she has determined, is hard to get: "And affection is a strange thing and much more rare than is supposed. It is possible that it exists within the bonds of marriage. It certainly is not to be found without them" (70).

Martin, the first of Enid Bagnold's important butler characters, tries to advise Serena. He is worldly, experienced, and cynical. He tells her after the unfortunate experience with Lord Ivor Cream, "A lady who stays to tea when she has been asked to luncheon . . . is never engaged to be married" (84).

Serena listens to (but has not been affected by) the countess's rules governing a young girl's behavior ". . . that nothing must be given away, not one fingertip. That lips must express every provocation but must not kiss. That eyes must look every assent during the coldest of denials" (126).

The irony is that dishonesty and hypocrisy are the methods that assure success, whereas Serena with her honesty and naturalness cannot be successful. When she has become engaged and all is, presumably, going well, she says: "How pleasant . . . is popularity. Poverty and failure produce no goodwill, but with a little triumph, a little success, one can purchase something very like kindness" (218).

Later, she speculates on another important philosophical truth: " 'The fortunes of a young woman are the most hazardous in the world,' she reflected. 'A man who makes money takes many years to make it, and even the few who inherit accidentally go many months. . . . But every young woman born on this earth may by chance find herself, at a word from a stranger, transplanted, transported, ruined, or offered a fortune' " (218–19). She bemoans the fact that a young woman can gain nothing by her merits and little by her own efforts, and that her future is an uncertain proposition.

Wit is present throughout and keeps one from becoming completely involved in Serena's fortunes and misfortunes. Still unsure of her success, she asks Martin if he knows why the count is marrying her. She says she would feel more secure if she knew. " God knows," Martin replies (216).

But this is the same Serena who near the beginning of the novel rejected the idea of working for a living: " 'It is not,' she thought, 'that bread is not easy to earn; but that it is not worth earning for a woman of my youth and beauty' " (19). In earning her bread she will lose her beauty, she feels, and then where will she find the fortune that belongs to her face?

In Martin's final advice when he points out the advantages of the match (also in stylized, balanced structure), he says of the count: "But he is rich . . . and willing to marry you. It is better to be married in Iberia than single in London. True, he is the illegitimate son of a Nicaraguan Indian woman by her first lover, a Spanish Creole. True he is not a count at all, and has no name beyond Montague, given him as a joke by his mother's second lover, an Englishman. But it is true too that his mother, though dark, was once a beauty and married an Argentine. Dying, he left his money equally between the mother and the adopted son" (229–30). The repetition of the word "true" humorously serves as a guide to the only important truth, that he has inherited money.

Labels are not always necessary, important, or even relevant. Whether *Serena Blandish* is a philosophical novel, whether ideas were suggested by *Candide,* it is a masterful piece of writing; on its own it is a mosaic of brilliant colors with enough original beauty and character so that it need not be compared to anything else; it is certainly a tour de force.

The Play

The diction in the novel is gemlike, precise, brilliant. The narrative passages are as stylized as the dialogue and necessary elements in the total effect; this is one reason why the play was not as successful as the novel.

The theatrical producer, Crosby Gaige, had suggested to American playwright S. N. Behrman that *Serena Blandish* might make a good play. Behrman read it and agreed. He sensed in Enid Bagnold a kindred spirit and, on a visit to London in 1928, arranged a meeting with her. The play opened in New York at the Morosco Theater on 4 February 1929 and played for ninety-three performances.

Behrman created a new character Edgar, Martin's son, and it is with Edgar that Serena runs off at the end of the play; therefore, the effect of the ending is quite different, nor is Serena's nature the same since she falls in love and becomes self-possessed. In the novel she is never self-possessed, nor ever falls in love, and at the end is still the victim and seemingly helpless in the events in which she takes part. These variations in the play result in a diminution of tone and irony.

In the foreword of Behrman's printed edition of the play he writes an "Apology to the Author of 'Serena Blandish'." He says in part: "As I read again, after an interval of four years, the novel from which this play is made, I am ravished again by its glamours and I see quite clearly why I yielded to the impossible temptation of transferring them to the theatre. Your book, so innocent and insidious, seduces one with the wish to have written it oneself.[3]

He acknowledges then the problem of the ending and the rationalization for his version of it, the fear of the public's nonacceptance of the racial elements. Serena's full-blooded Indian mother-in-law is dark-skinnned; "black" the narrative says.

In conclusion, the incident of the jeweler's loan of the diamond ring with the hope that sizable orders might follow, seems to have been suggested by an experience that Enid Bagnold had not long before she met her husband. She had tried on a beautiful fur coat in an expensive shop with no intention of buying or money to pay for it, but she had inquired if small payments could be made. The store owner, Mr. Reveille, told her she could have the coat for a five-dollar down payment if she would promise to buy her trousseau from him. When she said that she was not getting married and was not even engaged, he assured her that with that coat she would be engaged within a month. The proposition paid off. She took the coat and not long after she met and married Roderick Jones. She purchased her trousseau from Reveille in addition to another fur coat. The original coat, as it happens, cost eighty pounds, the same amount as the diamond ring in *Serena Blandish*.

Chapter Four

Novels of the Middle Years: Focus on the Family

National Velvet (1935)

The two novels discussed in this chapter are from the middle years of Enid Bagnold's life and take place in a village much like Rottingdean on the coast, her home for many years. Both are novels with an emphasis on family, but their protagonists differ markedly in age. In *National Velvet* the central character is Velvet, a girl of fourteen; in *The Squire* the major character is the mother of the family, nicknamed the Squire. While it may have been easy for Enid Bagnold to be the Squire at this time in her life, it is remarkable that she could so convincingly become Velvet, through whose eyes the story of *National Velvet* unfolds.

Clearly she remembered playing with the paper horses in Jamaica, her love of horses and riding stemming from those early days; now it was as the mother of the family that she experienced events often similar to those in the novel, with her daughter Laurian becoming a prototype for Velvet.

Rottingdean, apparently, had long been a horse-racing village. The property that Roderick Jones acquired included stalls (loose boxes) made of brick with iron mangers, but not until the groom McHardy joined the household were they put to use. McHardy, an ex-jockey, was the model for Mi Taylor, Velvet's friend and aid in winning the Grand National in the novel. He remained with the Joneses for ten years and became an essential part of the household, functioning as a groom and the focal point of all the equestrian activity, but apparently also much more.

Bagnold considered him more important than a governess. He involved the whole family in a commitment to horses and racing events. Eventually they owned thirteen ponies and spent many happy summers competing. All of the children participated but with varying degrees of interest. Laurian was the most serious rider, but even Dominick (Tucker) at five years of age rode and won prizes.

Bagnold admits that she hadn't intended to write a novel, only a story about a young girl and her love of a pony, but their family activities, the household pets, the antics of the children, and her own joyous emotions crowded into the pages, and the book evolved. She was proud of her children and their success.

Ironically, when the manuscript was finished, she asked Thayer Hobson, the president of William Morrow, Inc., the United States publisher, for an advance. He indicated that the story wouldn't sell in America but that it was charmingly written, and though it might not be a worthwhile financial venture, he could be indulgent in publishing it. Obviously he was wrong about its success. The book became a selection of the Book-of-the-Month Club in America and of the Book Society in England, several critics calling it a masterpiece. The book has gone through twenty-five printings in the U.S. and, no doubt, will go through many more. The movie and television versions made *National Velvet* even more famous. It was also presented as a play.

The plot of the novel is fanciful although the improbable elements are treated realistically. The Brown family of five children belong to the middle class; their father is a butcher, and the mother in her youth a celebrated channel swimmer. Velvet loves horses and has been riding since she was four on their one horse. In a village raffle she wins a piebald horse that has been jumping fences and escaping from his enclosure. By a strange quirk she also inherits five horses from an elderly landowner. The girls take care of the horses, and Velvet, inspired by Mi Taylor's stories of the Grand National, declares that she wants to ride the piebald in the big race.

Mi Taylor has had experience with training horses in the past but now he works for Mr. Brown in the slaughterhouse. Mi's father was Mrs. Brown's coach on her channel swim many years before. Mi agrees to help Velvet disguise herself as a boy, since girls are not allowed to enter the race, and to get the proper credentials as a participating jockey. The preparations and the race itself are sources of suspense. Velvet wins the race but falls from her horse soon after crossing the finish line. Her horse is disqualified, and the spectators with most of the English population are caught up in a wave of sentiment when they discover that the winning jockey is a girl of fourteen. Velvet and Mi are called to explain themselves before the Hunt Commission but are exonerated from charges of fraud. Her motive for entering the race, she says, was to give the deserving piebald fame and a history. Velvet's own fame makes life difficult for the family, but eventually the public enthusiasm disappears, and life goes back to normal.

Although there is no formal division, in the first section of the novel Enid Bagnold concentrates on the establishing of tone, setting, and character. In the second part plot becomes more important with the preparations for the Grand National, the actual race, and its aftermath; this part is, therefore, more suspenseful and faster moving than the earlier portion.

One of the charming elements of the novel is the atmosphere of warmth, family love, and wonder with a notable absence of cynicism or materialism, probably because one views the world through Velvet's eyes. Life, for her, is simple and relatively uncomplicated.

Local color is an important aspect of the book and expertly presented, partly through description of place and partly through the character of the dialogue. For instance, at the local gymkhana (program of racing competitions) rain makes the day dismal, and at this point there have been no winning entries for the family. Velvet and her sisters are competing in the various events on untrained horses. Edwina is annoyed, for she knows the horse she is riding, Mrs. James, will not perform as she should: " 'A lot of chance I have!' said Edwina. 'Mrs. James'll break every pole.' 'She gets rough and excited,' said Velvet. 'But it's Adults!' said Merry. 'They won't have nippy ponies. It'll be easier.'. . . But the Adults were seated on the smallest ponies they could ride. They looked like giants on dogs. Every grownup was riding his sister's pony and Mrs. James, galloping like a wild animal, nostrils blowing and eyes rolling, broke all the poles she could break. Edwina led her back without a word, disgusted and silent."[1]

At the intermission in the afternoon's activities Velvet reviews their losses. " 'It's the tea interval,' said Velvet gloomily. They had won nothing. They had made not a penny. They owed Mi thirty bob. . . . the rain slid, tapping, through the branches, and swept its windy puffs across the field" (*NV*, 149). But their spirits are lifted momentarily when they see their mother coming across the field in the red and yellow meat van. "She's brought tea!" said Merry (*NV*, 150).

Probably the strongest feature of the novel is the characterization.

Enid Bagnold's people live and are authentic. Even the animals are individualized, for she seems to understand the quirks and temperaments of horses and dogs especially.

She has also an ear for dialogue, a talent which is more apparent in *National Velvet* than in any of the other novels. Her style, for the first time, is realistic and conventional, in support perhaps of the lifestyle of ordinary people and the flavor of the community.

Velvet is not a young Elizabeth Taylor. While her sisters are described as three "golden greyhounds," she is spoken of as the plain one. She is imaginative and persistent. Mi Taylor sees in her the greatness that his father, the swimming coach, saw in Araminty Brown, the determination of the channel swimmer. She loves horses and devotes most of her waking moments fantasizing about them, caring for them, or riding. She has within a short time graduated from playing with the paper horses to managing six horses in addition to the original family horse, the thirteen-year-old Miss Ada. Earlier, when Miss Ada was the only one, Velvet had prayed, "Oh God, give me horses, give me horses! Let me be the best rider in England!" (*NV*, 18).

The quality that Mi Taylor especially values in Velvet is her willingness to consider the good of the horses first and to subordinate her own interests. One of these instances occurs during the gymkhana. The untrained piebald, although a natural jumper, has no experience with the hurdles of a race course: ". . . the piebald's jumping was a joke. Arrived at the jump in another two paces, he appeared to be astonished, planted his forelegs for a second, looked down, trembled, then leapt the little bush and rail with all four legs stiff in the air together. Dropping his hindquarters badly he came down on the rail and broke it in two" (*NV*, 145).

In the next hurdle, the In-and-Out, the horse, after jumping in, pauses and attempts to graze while the crowd laughs loudly. "She's handling him gentle," said Mi. "She's trying to keep him thinking he's a winner." After a few more errors around the course the horse approaches a wall: "He saw the friendly wall ahead, and taking it to be enduring flint he went for it with a glare of interest, ears pricked, and eyes bright. The wall was three foot six. He leapt five. For a second it seemed to the crowd as though the horse had nothing to do with the wall but was away up in the air. A little cheer went up and hands clapped in a burst. 'Don't she ride him!' said the voice. 'It's that Velvet girl. The ugly one' " (*NV*, 145–46).

Velvet does not attempt to complete the round, the last jump. Later, when her sister Mally asks why, Velvet answers gently, "I thought I'd better not . . . He did the wall so beautifully I thought he'd better end on that" (*NV,* 147). Her concern for the piebald is evident also at the end of the novel when a moviemaker wishes to use the horse for a film. Velvet refuses; she does not want him to be exploited.

Entering the piebald in the Grand National is Velvet's idea, but Mi approves. An author's note in the 1975 edition of the novel tells us that in steeplechase races before 1931 it was not necessary for a horse to have a distinguished racing record and that, with no specifications, she assumes, even "a zebra could have entered, provided he was the proper age" (*NV,* 307).

Velvet and Mi are not considering the money or the actual honor of winning. They know that if Velvet is able to disguise herself as a boy in order to enter the race, she will be disqualified when they discover that she isn't. The challenge of winning and of allowing the piebald to show what he can do, these are the motives for making the effort. Mi is confident that Velvet can do well.

There has been a certain mystery about Mi's past, as there was in the real life of McHardy, but the reader is surprised to discover during the Hunt Commission hearing that Mi Taylor does not "ride"; however his loyalty and ingenuity have made it possible for Velvet to be in the Grand National.

Velvet's mother, Araminty Brown, is supportive when Velvet tells her what she hopes to do and offers the registration fee that Mi must bring ahead of time. She decides that it would be appropriate to use the gold coins, the sovereigns, the prize money she won at nineteen and saved over the years; and, after some confusion on the part of the officials, the entry fee of gold is accepted. Velvet's mother knows about courage and endurance. She is now a heavy woman, quiet and strong, aiding in the butcher shop adjacent to the house, doing the accounts, and acting as cashier. The children adore her.

Mr. Brown is the head of the family and keeps his position with dignity; he is not as inclined to give consent when he is finally told of Velvet's venture, but Mrs. Brown persuades him; he is, of course, as proud of Velvet as the rest of the family when she succeeds.

Velvet's sisters are also involved in caring for the horses, but each has her own special outside interest. Meredith keeps pet canaries.

Little Donald, Velvet's only brother, is a principal source of humor in the novel; he is well adjusted and firmly handled by his mother but as eccentric as many four-year-olds can be. He carries with him a medicine bottle on a string. "It's my spit bottle," he says. "He's collecting his spit," says Velvet to Mr. Croom, the grocer, who has come in for coffee on the day she inherits the horses (*NV,* 89). A few days later Donald falls on the top step and smashes his bottle: "It had been the work of weeks. The stairs ran with spit and blood and tinkled with broken glass. The house was rent" (*NV,* 121–22). Luckily, aside from a stitch in the ball of his foot, Donald sustains no serious injuries. Obviously Enid Bagnold's experiences within her own family have made her an expert on the nuances and details that make these characters believable.

As suggested previously, even the animals have definite personalities. This is especially true of the horse Miss Ada, the piebald, and of Jacob, the old fox terrier. Approximately two pages of description are reserved for Jacob. One is told that "the Browns loved Jacob as they loved each other, deeply, from the back of the soul, with intolerance in daily life" (*NV,* 8).

Authentic detail is present in the description of the preliminary steps, the physical preparations that Mi and Velvet take, leading to the beginning of the Grand National race. At race time, the weather is rainy and a heavy mist blows in. Because the reader is now with Mi rather than Velvet, one does not know exactly what is happening in the race. Mi's vision is limited as he tries desperately to follow Velvet's progress. Horses stumble or riders fall, but he cannot tell who is in difficulty. Suspense mounts and remains intense until after the race is finished, and at first most of the crowd cannot tell who has won. Then Mi sees the piebald galloping riderless and runs to catch him. He is distraught at first until he finds that Velvet is unharmed and that the piebald is indeed the winner. The fact that the horse is disqualified later does not matter.

The ending of the novel, after the enormous publicity surrounding Velvet, is handled well and realistically. The story does not end at the height of glory, as it might have, but after the public has already forgotten the event. Velvet has not been affected by the public adulation; she and the rest of the family feel only relief when they are allowed to live in peace and go on with their lives. In that respect, the ending is anticlimactic but much more satisfying than if the author had left Velvet at the height of fame.

It is a mistake to think of *National Velvet* as only a children's book.

It is no more exclusively a children's book than are *Kidnapped, Treasure Island, Robinson Crusoe, Gulliver's Travels,* or *Oliver Twist.* These novels may have fanciful elements, but they have become classics largely because of superb characterization and deft handling of plot and detail. Their authors are masterful storytellers who have much to say to adults as well as children about life and the human condition.

Of the book, Lewis Gannett in the *New York Herald Tribune* of 26 April 1935, said: " 'National Velvet' is a book to buy, to read, to remember and to talk about, and to keep instead of lending." Christopher Morley in the *Saturday Review of Literature* (4 May 1935) had said: "For those who can ride the flying trapeze of fancy, this is a masterpiece. Should we say something solemn and sociological? Very well then; you can learn more about the mind of childhood from this book than from many volumes of pedagogy. The mind of childhood, zigzag, indolent, unblemished by the subjunctive mood, is the mind of any great artist."

The role of Velvet was Elizabeth Taylor's first major screen part and the one that made her a star. She was eleven years old when MGM first considered her for the lead in the film, but studio officials said she was too small. According to the biography *Elizabeth Taylor: The Last Star,* producer Pandro S. Berman decided to wait for her to grow. She was given riding lessons, and in her enthusiasm to play the part, Elizabeth began collecting horse pictures and other articles dealing with riding. She also began calling herself Velvet. "National Velvet was really me," she said years later.[2]

Finally, when Elizabeth was twelve, shooting began; the picture was filmed in seven months. She was required to wear braces on her teeth as Velvet did in the novel and also a wig because Elizabeth's father refused to let the studio cut her hair to make her look like a boy for the racing sequence.

In appreciation of her performance in the smash hit the studio gave Elizabeth the horse she had ridden, King Charles, in addition to a bonus of $15,000.[3] Mickey Rooney had played Mi Taylor, and Anne Revere, as Mrs. Brown, had won an Oscar for best supporting actress. Like the novel, the film (1944) is still receiving attention. The television networks show it periodically.

In 1946 Enid Bagnold's adaptation of *National Velvet* opened at the Embassy Theatre in London, but as a play it could not capture the charm or the life of the novel.

The Squire (1938)

The Squire was called *The Door of Life* when it first appeared in 1938. The present title comes from the leading character, not a man as might be expected, but a woman temporarily the head of her household while her husband is on a three-month business trip to India.

Bagnold narrows the scope of time, place, and action to a six-week period in a locale more limited than that of *National Velvet*. The village is still Rottingdean but now the focus is within the house and garden of an upper-class English family, much like her own. With all action taking place here and almost no intrusion from the outside, the author creates a sheltered existence for her characters, a temporary retreat, suitable for the main event, the birth of the family's fifth child.

Plot is not the major element of the book. Little happens from beginning to end externally, but much develops internally in preparation for the big event and the weeks thereafter. Actually, the birth affects the rest of the household very little. The other children go on with their daily activities while the children's nurse and the rest of the staff see that they are well taken care of; at the same time, they are aware of their mother's presence, even when she is secluded with the newest family member.

As the novel begins, the squire is awaiting the imminent birth, and soon the midwife arrives; she remains then for two weeks to oversee the care of the new baby. The household is complicated by its service structure of parlor, kitchen, and nursemaids, besides a cook, butler, and regular children's nurse, in addition to a groom and gardener, whom one never sees; add to this four children, three boys and a girl, ranging in age from four to ten, and one can see that the squire, while theoretically a lady of leisure, is in reality a woman with much responsibility.

Two days before the baby is born, the squire fires the regular cook and hires a Mrs. Lynch. Then, after the birth, she hibernates for two weeks in the upper regions of the house, trusting that the household routine will remain intact, operating smoothly. It does after a fashion, but partly because the midwife manages enough control to fire the recently hired cook, Mrs. Lynch, who does not show up for breakfast because she is sleeping off a hangover: " 'You must leave, Mrs. Lynch' said the midwife, without preamble." Asked why, she says

"Because what you do threatens my work. A baby has been born in this house. If you cannot understand what that means you must go."[4]

Within two days the midwife hires a new cook, a good worker, quiet, a Scotch woman who knows her job. The squire, willing to laugh at herself and her lack of skill in judging the character of a good cook offers an explanation of why she hired Mrs. Lynch in the first place: " 'A woman offers herself, wearing some strange mask which she keeps on for a while. One has twenty minutes to decide and few alternatives. I thought her cold, still look meant efficiency. I thought her icy eye meant she could manage the kitchenmaid. She was neat. She carried a little case. She looked like a secretary.' 'You should get them when they look like cooks,' said the midwife mildly" (*S*, 301).

The servant problem is one of the main sources of humor in this story, and touches of wit are present throughout, in characterization and in dialogue. The novel is serious, however, and the humor only incidental. It is a philosophical novel in that the squire examines the complicated issues of birth, the satisfactions of her own life at this stage—she is now forty-four—while acknowledging and being ever conscious of the presence of death. She has little faith in the possibility of a hereafter and her musings are not religious in nature. She can be impatient and argumentative; at the same time she is positive, optimistic, strong, courageous, self-reliant—qualities of the sturdy mother figure, reminiscent of Mrs. Brown in *National Velvet* and like Enid Bagnold herself.

The squire has a sense of humor, and her imperfections are as obvious to herself as to the rest of the household. She sees herself now as a vehicle, a pipeline between the past and the future, in the long line of women responsible for fulfilling their role in the human race.

Much is made of the contrast between the romantic, passionate love of woman for her lover and the strong, satisfying maternal love of the mother for her child. In this respect the squire and her friend Lady Caroline are foils. Lady Caroline, fifteen years her junior, is the only person from the outside world, aside from the new servants, who visits the squire. Caroline lives across the green and is in the area only for the summer, as a retreat of another sort. Caroline is beautiful, worldly, egoistic, anxious to discuss with the squire her current romantic love. In Caroline the squire sees herself as she once was, and she finds her own maternal involvement much more satisfying than the passion and excitement she hardly remembers from earlier years, emotions which will never come again. Her present stage she considers an advancement, a result of maturity, experience, loss of selfish desires, and increased wisdom. Her attitude toward Caroline, therefore, is somewhat patronizing.

In one scene Lady Caroline has come to lunch and they talk, mostly about her love complications, although the reader is never allowed to know what those are. At two o'clock the nurse interrupts them to bring in the baby for its breast feeding. The squire requests Caroline to continue the conversation, as she holds the infant in her lap: "With her lover in her lap she listened to the visitor telling of hers. Love all at once seemed to the mother indescribably stale . . . When the baby had been taken away the light went out of the room. That emptied vase which was the mother turned again to her visitor" (S, 336).

Earlier, as she holds the new baby, she feels the superiority of their mother/child relationship over all others: "In all relationships that she had hitherto known, in childhood, in friendship, in love, in mating, the partner fought, the partner struggled to live, to command, to break away or to break in. But here for a short while she held in her arms the perfect companion. . ." (S, 296).

The squire is ultimately satisfied with her home, her five children, and the merchant/husband. This is his first absence during the birth of one of their children, but she welcomes this opportunity to concentrate on the event and to sort out her own feelings. It would seem that the father has been too conveniently taken out of the way, for there is no strong sense of his presence in the family, no continuity of relationship. At the beginning of the last chapter one finds that he is on his way home. That is the extent of information about the permanent squire. Otherwise, he is mentioned only briefly at the beginning and twice during the novel. One never knows his name, the lady squire's real name, or even the family's name. As in *The Happy Foreigner,* one lives in the moment with no details to tie one to past history or the family's activities once this special time is over; yet the characters are real. One tends to believe in them as possible members of Enid Bagnold's own family.

The youngest member before the baby arrives is four-year-old Henry. He reminds one of Donald in *National Velvet.* Boniface is seven, Jay eight or nine, and Lucy is ten. Their interests are normal, and their relationship with their mother warm and loving. Obviously they feel secure within the family. They play with animal-like exuberance.

Although minor household crises temporarily disturb the squire's tranquillity, she manages to cope with the problems. She can change fuses, deal with the nursery maid caught stealing, or fire the alcoholic butler Crutchley who passes out at the dining room table.

Crutchley is only temporary, but he is more amiable than Pratt, the family decides. The squire thinks he looks almost monastic: "Knowing his job, swift and fat, sliding through passages with a curious walk. He looked like a bald and nimble bishop, with a watch-chain where the cross should have lain. . . . 'Mr. Crutchley smells sweet and cold,' said Boniface. 'It seems like eau-de-Cologne,' said the squire. . ." (*S*, 333). The overwhelming odor continues as Crutchley serves dinner: "Crutchley moved about, tiptoeing oddly. . . .'Mr. Crutchley's drunk,' said Boniface, firm and loud. Crutchley made no response. If indeed he heard at all. . ." (*S*, 342). After dinner he serves coffee to the squire in the courtyard, carrying out the silver tray and placing it on the courtyard table. Then he walks carefully back to the dining room and passes out in the squire's chair.

The regular butler Pratt has been an important member of the household for twelve years; not always helpful, he avoids unpleasantness and, though of the old order of servants, maintains an untidy pantry. He respects the squire but dislikes women in general. One senses that he, like the butler in *The Chalk Garden,* has been patterned after Cutmore, the Joneses' family butler for many years. Pratt, unlike Crutchley, is aware of the dangers of drink and he knows his limits.

The household structure forms an important part of the novel; for this reason Enid Bagnold uses the multiple point of view. The novel begins with the reactions of the servants to the coming event, and at strategic points throughout the book the viewpoint shifts from the squire to the servants. The narrative technique, however, remains somewhat impressionistic in that there is little sense of history or explanation for present events.

More use is made of imagery than in previous novels. Since the village is on the seacoast, one finds many sea and water references: e.g., "The baby seemed to swim and strike like a dolphin" (259); phrases such as "sea-deep content" or "sea-deep peace." At one point the village itself seems like a ship: "The village green outside was white with moonlight. As she stepped on to it it seemed a deck, her village ship a-sail on the slant of the world" (S, 235).

The squire sees in her son Boniface conflicts like tides: "Under his factual life there were winds veering and blowing, tides pulling, tides ebbing" (S, 262). In describing the pain-sensation of childbirth the squire thinks of a river: ". . . But there comes a time, after the first pains have passed, when you swim down a silver river running like a torrent, with the convulsive, corkscrew movements of a great fish, threshing from its neck to its tail. And if you can *marry* the movements, go with them, turn like a screw in the river and swim on, then the pain . . . then I believe the pain . . . becomes a flame which doesn't burn you" (S, 266). And again, in the midst of the pains she concentrates on her part in the process: "And now she spoke no more, only savouring her moments of release; waiting for the sea to heave her from her beach and drown her in its pressure of black violence" (S, 288).

Growth images and plant images are plentiful also. Most evident, surprisingly, are the references to death or dying. There are at least fifty-one such words or passages, and yet these allusions and philosophical musings do not affect the positive tone of the novel. Their handling is delicate, and they remain in the background. Also, the squire has such zest for living that it is difficult to take her fears seriously. She appears too stable and too active to be much affected by shadows; she considers the power of the birth process in dispelling fear: "How strangely the birth of a baby pressed away the menace of death and assuaged in the breast that savage and pitiful need for immortality!" (S, 293). Again, she says, "But a child in the womb or at the breast stops time. Time stands still. Death recedes. All this she knew" (S, 293).

For the squire this summer is a special time, and once the autumn and winter set in, the joy of life and the regular round of family activities will envelop her and blur the emotions felt so deeply now.

The close relationship between the squire and the midwife is akin to a religious experience; sometimes the squire thinks of the doctor and nurse as the "monk" and "nun." The midwife considers hers a mystic connection with the newborn; she strives for perfect conditions, certain that good beginnings strongly influence physical and emotional growth; thus, the squire gives herself up to the direction of the midwife with absolute trust.

Of Enid Bagnold's novels, *The Squire* has been the least popular, perhaps in part because its subject matter appeals more to women. Nevertheless, Heinemann Publishers considered the book important enough to print again in 1954, this time with *The Happy Foreigner* in a volume called *The Girl's Journey.*

When Noel Coward was residing in Jamaica, he found leisure time for reading. In his diary he records the pleasures of reading *The Happy Foreigner* and *The Squire:* ". . . I have read about eight books since I arrived, including *The Happy Foreigner* and *The Squire* by Enid Bagnold. Both exquisitely written. She really is an extraordinary writer and her use of English is magical."[5]

Chapter Five

The Autumn Years: A Novel of Maturity and Endings

The Loved and Envied (1951)

Much happened in the years between the publication of *The Squire* (1938) and the appearance of the new novel. World War II had created changes within the family and crises within the economic structure of the country. Enid Bagnold had become involved with the theater and had written two plays with some success, *Lottie Dundass* (1941) and *Poor Judas* (1946) (see next chapter). *The Loved and Envied* was to be her last novel. From then on she considered the drama more challenging and concentrated on becoming a playwright.

The writing of this novel, from the earliest idea to the finished work, spanned a ten-year period. She says in the *Autobiography* that MGM had asked her to write a movie script about a heroine who would be more mature than the average screen star, between the ages of forty and fifty, they said. The rewards would have been great. She was offered a large sum of money and the contract was drawn up, but no inspiration came, only guilt about not carrying through with the bargain. Finally she sent the papers back and, relieved of the pressure, found herself able to write.

She created as the central figure a woman of legendary beauty, impeccable character, and a gift for friendship, patterned after her friend Diana Manners Cooper. She says admiringly of Diana: ". . . She puts friendship above everything, that is her gift of gifts. No catastrophe so black but she wouldn't tackle it. Go to prison and she'd have you out. Shame doesn't upset her . . . When you are her friend you are socially made, but no one would be her friend who thought it. . ." (*A*, 282).

Like Ruby in *The Loved and Envied*, Diana early in her career had been an actress. In later years, when she and Bagnold had become friends, her husband was British ambassador to France, and the author often went over from England to stay with her. Noel Coward and Evelyn Waugh were also among Diana's good friends. Bagnold had seen Diana for the first time at a party at Catherine d'Erlanger's house in London and had been much impressed. Diana had a magnetic personality and electric blue eyes; people gravitated toward her.

In the novel Lady Ruby Maclean has a similar effect on those around her. At the opening of the book she is fifty-three, still amazingly attractive but on the edge of losing the power and the magnetism. The gift for friendship she will presumably never lose nor her enthusiasm for life. Over the years she has been the "loved and envied."

This work differs from Bagnold's others in several ways. For the first time her people have a history, a definite past. One knows about them, experiencing events through the eyes of many characters, viewing them in relation to each other and in their attachment to the main figure, Ruby.

The members of this special group are well-to-do, in some cases aristocratic, people living in a countrified suburb of Paris, the Forest of Bas-Pouilly; some have homes also in Paris and elsewhere. The group is unusual in that several are transplants, not native Frenchmen; among them with the French are Englishmen, an American, and an Italian. During the course of the novel, although the focus is on the Bas-Pouilly area, the reader finds himself through flashbacks in England, Scotland, other sections of France, and in Jamaica.

The author explores the childhood of various characters; otherwise she presents them in two main periods: in the present and at a point in their lives eight years before. In part 1 of the book one learns their histories and begins to experience the endings of death or separation; and in part 2, in the present, more characters "leave" while those left behind prepare to resume their lives.

Another major difference in this novel lies in the age of the characters. As *The Squire* is a story of the middle years, *The Loved and Envied* is the saga of the later years, most of Bagnold's people being in their sixties and seventies. (She, herself, at the publication of this book was sixty-one years old.) These people have been loyal friends for many years, and now they must adjust to the losses of love and friendship. Yet the book is not depressing; on the whole, the characters have enjoyed their lives and accept what comes. Loneliness later becomes a problem that is not always resolved.

Characterization

The plot of the novel is less significant than its characterization. As in the other works, the people are real to the reader. The story revolves around five major couples: Edouard, the Vicomte de Bas-Pouilly, and his mistress Rose; Alberti, the Duca di Roccafergolo, and his housekeeper Celestine; Cora and Rudi Holbein; Miranda, Ruby's daughter, and her husband Tuxie (later replaced by James); and Lady Ruby and Sir Gynt Maclean. Besides these, several characters appear briefly; for example, Edouard's sister Angel de Lison who resents her brother's mistress of thirty-three years but has never seen her.

Edouard de Bas-Pouilly may have been patterned after Enid's Uncle Lex, a wealthy barrister with beautiful manners who remained unmarried because his mother on her deathbed had begged him to look after his (ugly) sister. He had never married therefore, but took a mistress and remained loyal and loving to her. Edouard stays with his sister three days a week in Paris, spends two days with Rose in their apartment, and then goes to the suburbs for the weekend to the forest of the Bas-Pouilly area (most of which he owns), where Ruby, Gynt, and Alberti live and are friends of his. At the opening of the novel he is seventy and Rose is sixty. Halfway through the novel, one day Edouard dies suddenly of a brain hemorrhage as he leans over to tie his shoe. Ruby goes to Paris to break the news to Rose and brings her back to Bas-Pouilly with her, but Rose dies of a broken heart a few days later, having nothing now to live for. One of the most bizarre incidents occurs when Edouard's sister comes to Bas-Pouilly, discovers that Rose has just died, and insists on satisfying her curiosity to see what Edouard's mistress looks like.

Alberti, the Duca de Roccafergolo, with an American mother and Italian father, seems to have been patterned after Enid Bagnold's friend Count Albrecht Bernstorff, a counselor at the German Embassy. He was a huge, whalelike man, full of laughter and with a love of the English, having spent happy years attending Oxford. Alberti, however, is shy and lives alone now at age seventy, except for his housekeeper, Celestine. He has been ill with dropsy and agrees to marry the housekeeper, a countrywoman from a small village, so that she can call herself the wife of a duke (which she craves). But he wishes her to be like a nanny to him, someone to call in the night to be at his bedside in the illness which now is fatal. He is afraid to be left alone at night or to die alone. At the end of the novel he dies and leaves to Ruby, whom he has loved for years, the bulk of his enormous estate. The inheritance, Alberti says, will provide a new life for Ruby who also finds herself alone at the end of the story.

Another couple, Cora and Rudi Holbein, were married years before but now have been divorced for over twenty years. Once a successful playwright, he is now no longer fashionable; at seventy, after sixty-four plays, he is ending his career, empty and lonely. He wants to be reconciled with Cora. She is an American, was married early to Rudi in Paris and was for a time a dutiful wife; later, detesting Rudi who neglected her, she left him; at present she enjoys her independence, her success as a painter, and lesbian relationships. She will not consider remarrying Rudi even though she is the only person who understands him. Their only son hates them both. Rudi has relied on Ruby's friendship during the trying time of his play's failure and the obvious ending of his career.

Miranda is Ruby and Gynt's daughter. She is now thirty-one and has just suffered through eight years of a disastrous marriage to Tuxie, a young man of shabby character, a fortune hunter. They have been living in Jamaica on Ruby's family plantation where Tuxie has been the overseer. They were trapped there by World War II and had not intended to stay in Jamaica so long. Earlier, Tuxie has been in love with Ruby and cannot understand why Miranda, silent and sullen, is so unlike her mother. He resents his exile, and one day in a rage as he is using a machete to chop down banana plants, he accidentally strikes the back of his leg and dies from loss of blood.

Miranda comes back to Bas-Pouilly still envying and not understanding her mother. Through Alberti, she meets a wealthy fashion designer, a homosexual who can see advantages to a marriage with Miranda, both for himself and for her. She accepts but is saved from another disastrous marriage by James, the heir to the Bas-Pouilly inheritance. James is only twenty-eight; he too has been in love with Ruby without encouragement; now he realizes that he loves and wants to marry Miranda. James and Miranda are the only young people in the group. As they begin a marriage and a hopeful future, they form a contrast to the aging characters about to end their careers and lives.

Ruby and Gynt Maclean are the main characters, although after one meets Gynt in the courtship days in England, one sees little of him. His ancestors are Scottish, but he has a French mother who gave the newly married couple a present of the house at Bas-Pouilly where they have lived for the past thirty-five years. Ruby's gaiety and "gift for friendship" have made her the focal point of their group and well known in society. Gynt now is becoming increasingly introspective and isolated. He is interested in birds and finishes a book about them; he is a sensitive man, more social in the past than he is now. When James arrives after several years' absence, he notes the change in Gynt. He has remembered him as a very lively man. Ruby admits, however, that Gynt has become deeply affected by the prospect of growing old.

James is surprised that getting old does not come naturally. Ruby says of Gynt: "He watches eternity as though it were a sea to cross and he Columbus. And I, you see, never lift my eyes from the island we live on together. I hardly know it's an island. That makes a barrier."[1] The barrier is between Ruby and Gynt. Gynt has strong mystic tendencies and wants to clarify his relationship with God; therefore he leaves for the East on his quest. He may never return. Gynt does not blame Ruby but obviously their relationship has not been meaningful enough nor their communication strong enough to keep them attuned to each other's needs.

Miranda and James are to move to the south of France, and with Edouard and Alberti gone, Ruby's life suddenly seems empty. She is not spiritual and does not have a religious faith nor the consolations that Alberti finds in his Catholicism.

One knows less about Gynt than about the other characters; he is therefore more mysterious, and one never shares the development of his religious experience. The announcement that he is leaving comes as a surprise to the reader as well as to Ruby. Ruby tells Alberti that it seems as if God has caught Gynt unaware in the woods and commands him to follow Him and to leave her. Alberti doesn't believe God plays such tricks and wonders why she can't join Gynt. Ruby confesses then that she hasn't the faith and is an outsider in respect to God.

Ruby feels guilt over Gynt's estrangement as she has in the past over her lack of communication with Miranda; though Ruby has not been conscious of it, envy of her mother has been a source of Miranda's problem. Now she asks her mother why everybody loves Ruby and no one loves Miranda. This is the first time that Miranda has tried to talk seriously with her mother, and it is a turning point in their relationship. Ruby is hurt but grateful for the effort. She responds by explaining that young men are often affected by their hostesses. They don't love her but enjoy being with her. This is part of an elderly woman's power and what is left when one is too old for love.

Ruby grew up in Jamaica; at sixteen, on the death of her father, she came to England with her mother. During the first winter there her mother died of pneumonia, and Ruby's education and career were taken over by her Aunt Ursula, an eccentric woman with a successful cosmetic business, although she herself has a facial disfigurement hidden by scarves. Ursula immediately sees Ruby's possibilities, for the young girl is beautiful and enjoys people. Ursula feels that she can give Ruby self-confidence and suggests a stage career. Ruby takes acting lessons for several months and does get a small acting role, but she does not have the talent or inclination to be an actress. In the meantime Gynt has seen her in London, followed her home, and sought the help of his mother to invite Ruby to their home in Scotland to which Lady Maclean is returning after closing their London house. Ursula allows Ruby to accept the invitation; thereafter, Gynt proposes, and following a short engagement, they are married, settling in the house in France. World War I separates Ruby and Gynt for a time, and there is the birth of their first child, a little boy who dies. All of these events have affected Ruby, but her outer face remains the same, smiling and friendly. She continues to be the most vibrant and dynamic individual in their set.

Aside from the account of Miranda and her own growing up, one does not experience the busy social lives of Ruby and Gynt or Ruby's success as a society figure and hostess. The story resumes in the present when Ruby is fifty-three years old and Miranda comes back from Jamaica after the death of Tuxie.

The Aura Is Fading

At the beginning of the novel Edouard's mistress Rose has seen Ruby Maclean from afar, at the theater; she has heard of Ruby for years and been envious of her. She complains to Edouard that in spite of what's happened to the world and to all of them, Ruby still has everything. Rose believes that it comes from living in a tight secluded circle; so powerful and beloved has Ruby become that she is now a myth; and everyone is determined that Ruby should be unassailable. In the beginning it was because of her beauty but the mystique is still there although now she is between fifty and sixty years old; her admirers don't seem to notice that their queen is turning gray.

Later, experiencing Ruby's kindness on the death of Edouard, Rose feels differently. The envy becomes gratitude for the extended friendship.

Cora Holbein, the successful artist, has confided to Ruby that ugly women can have love but what she wants to feel is admiration. Cora would sell her soul to the devil if she could walk out now and look as Ruby does. As Ruby's friend, she can accept the advantage Ruby has had and not be bitter, for she has her fame as an artist.

Ruby's influence has grown over the years as a result of beauty, personality, and then friendship. The reader encounters her now, however, in a more passive, retiring role and must accept the judgments of the other characters in regard to her influence. The attention is not so much on the character of Ruby as on the attitudes of the others toward themselves and their lives. Now comes the tallying up, the realization of emptiness, in some cases, defeat. Rose bemoans the loss of her looks and that Edouard has never married her. Rudi regrets that he did not provide time for love and a happy marriage. Alberti realizes that with all of his money he has no one to be with in the night or to console him in his illness. Gynt knows that he must pursue a spiritual relationship with God. Ruby, too, must make a sudden reassessment. Her own financial situation has always been assured, but instead of retiring quietly by herself, she now has the challenge of managing a huge fortune, of meeting new people and redirecting her life. She has lost her husband, her greatest admirer, and some of the friends who have been an essential part of her life. Although her attitude remains positive, it seems to the reader that Ruby is not entirely enthusiastic about the future. She will, no doubt, carry on and survive well but with less satisfaction and less heart.

Moments of Revelation

Throughout the novel occasions arise when characters discover certain truths; these moments of revelation are important and affect the way these people see themselves and the world. Some discoveries are minor but others are of prime importance. Enid Bagnold is especially effective in the depiction of these experiences. Underlying the serious matter are often touches of humor and always vivid diction.

On the opening night of Rudi's play, an event mentioned several times during the course of the novel as a point of reference, Ruby sits looking about her, sad about the failure of the play and the audience's lack of response. She realizes suddenly how unsparingly unkind their world is. As she looks around again, she is struck by the numbers of old people in the moneyed seats, people whose faces reflect spite and power. She sees now that, in Paris at least, the old are not weaponless and are not to be pitied.

Also, the elderly are not always the forgotten. These people in the audience are not in the same category with her own friends who are compassionate and vulnerable. Rudi, she knows, is outstaying his popular acceptance as a playwright, but fashionable audiences still appear at his plays even if to scoff; unfortunately, he has become so mechanical and predictable that he writes "like a machine left running at the door while the master, the soul, was away on another errand" (88). Rudi has repeated the same pattern in all of his plays, and this is to be the last.

Later, Ruby is suddenly aware that all of her men friends are getting older. She is shaken by Alberti's loneliness. She feels pity for all those people unable to cope with the arrival of age. She has always believed that men accepted aging more readily, but she knows now that it is easier for women.

This is a truth with which Rose, Edouard's mistress, does not agree. It is not easier for women! Suddenly Rose is obsessed with the idea of studying other old people; in the process of this particular moment of revelation she also watches herself as she passes reflecting windows. She sees a sad, coquettish old woman, and she considers herself now in that poor army of ugly women. She seats herself then on the terrace of a small cafe and in despair concentrates on the women in the street. Some of the ugly ones do have pride, she sees, but they have always been plain and have never experienced the beauty that she had. In fact, the really aged women are not in the streets at midday, but in their homes, shaded and quiet and secure.

Rose comments on the heat as she sits down next to a woman older than she in the park. The lady replies that that is one of the advantages of being old, that although she used to mind the heat, she no longer feels it. Rose is surprised that there are advantages, and she asks what the other advantages of being old are. The lady replies that now she is not so busy and has more time for herself, also that now she receives consideration from her family. She has five grown sons.

" 'My case is quite different,' said poor Rose, seeing at once how life ought to have gone (but then one doesn't map out one's whole life in preparation for age.) 'I've never had any children and I've never had anything at all to do' " (142). The older lady can not seem to comprehend such a life. Rose smiles at her and moves away. She feels she has had no consideration and wonders if had she followed through with her painting, things would have been different; but she knows how many would-be artists have been destroyed by lack of talent, by the demands of living and the passing years. She doesn't suppose she would have been lucky, but she suddenly realizes that she has had no respect from anyone but Edouard. It was unlucky to have been a mistress and not a wife all these years, especially after the age of fifty. She wonders then why Edouard couldn't have married her and decides that his sister was no doubt the reason. She sees now, however, that she has been too humble and, since Edouard has loved her enough to stay with her all his life, she might still ask for marriage. Ironically, just as Rose has made the decision to press for marriage, Edouard dies.

Edouard's sister, Angel de Lison, has been curious all these years about Rose and is horribly disappointed to find in arriving at Ruby's home that, not long after Edouard, Rose too died. The coffin is being carried out. In anger and frustration she tells Ruby that she has wanted to see Rose for years but Edouard would never let her. She wants to see Rose now before she is buried.

She wants the coffin lid unscrewed. The undertaker objects, but Ruby, taken aback by the violence of Angel's emotions, persuades him to open the wooden box:

"I shall choke if I don't see her.". . . two men began to undo the lid with their screwdrivers. Madame de Lison, breathing hard, took a step forward and another till she reached the door. When the lid was lifted, Rose, pale at last, appeared again among the legendary white ruchings.

"But she's OLD!" cried Edouard's sister in a loud voice of disbelief across the coffin to Ruby.

"Women get old," said Ruby. . . .

"What could have bound him to her?"

"I imagine—love."

"Love!" cried Angel de Lison, so sharply that the trestle tilted on the uneven floor . . . "And do you suppose" she asked in tones that fear made ringing, "she could once have been pretty?" (192)

Ruby wonders what Angel could have expected since good looks do not last forever. She asks Angel how she will look some day when she is done up in white satin and "carried in a box like an old doll?" (192).

In several of these revelations one can see evidence of Bagnold's special sense of humor. James, Edouard's twenty-eight-year-old nephew and heir, has at least two moments of revelation: when he realizes that his love for Ruby is gone and when he realizes that he wants to marry Ruby's daughter Miranda.

He has been infatuated with Ruby since he was a young boy, and now when he comes again to visit at Bas-Pouilly, he does not notice at first that she is older or that much of the magnetism is gone. Later, however, he becomes aware of Miranda, and when Ruby suggests to him that Miranda might be involved with Afric, the dress designer, he is annoyed. Ruby refers to the fact that Afric is a known homosexual, but James realizes then that his infatuation for Ruby is gone. He feels antagonistic to her mood. She is too far removed from him, and he sees that she looks older now; he knows that she has suffered since Gynt went away.

Thereafter, as he is talking to his aunt, Angel de Lison, almost without realizing what he is saying, he tells her that he is going to ask Miranda to marry him. He has not until that moment considered that he was in love. She is surprised:

It was the wildest, rashest piece of instinctive swimming he had ever done. He had made up his mind without thinking of it. He could hardly believe he had said it. It was one of those tranced executive moves which bring corporals to fame and turn them into generals.
"Does she know?" breathed Madame de Lison.
"No."
"So you'll be engaged tomorrow?"
"Only if she agrees." He got up quickly. He had to recover from his own choking surprise. (243–44)

Miranda's revelations come later. Enid Bagnold creates suspense as she opens chapter 28 with the words: "Now Miranda was to have two proposals on one day: and to accept the first" (247). Lewis Afric in Paris takes her to lunch and proposes. He admits to her that though he has a "friend" named Charles and that he is older than she (he is fifty-three), she would have many advantages as his wife. She would be the important person on whom he would build his affections. He wishes his mother were alive to reassure her. Miranda had not expected a proposal and is intrigued by the unusual circumstances. She realizes that he thinks her unsexed; on the other hand, she considers herself more of a woman than her mother, and this marriage may bring her a new chance in the future.

He tells her also that he can give her a career. Miranda appears calm, but she is panicky. Nothing seems to go simply in her life. Afric, on the other hand, is not in the least perturbed. He goes on eating as if he has just suggested a merger between the houses of Afric and Christian Dior.

When she asks him what his real name is, he tells her that he is Armenian and that if she doesn't know what a man's nationality is but believes he may not be proud of it, he's an Armenian. He says, "My name is Snosvic and so will be yours on your passport. You were right to ask" (251). Bagnold's wit surfaces often in unlikely places. The narrative continues: "He pushed his plate an inch away, he looked hard and defeated; for the moment he looked a very real man. Miranda took one of her swift decisions, making up her mind, as with Tuxie, rapidly and wrongly" (251). In his joy Afric takes her to Cartier's where he buys an expensive sapphire ring.

That afternoon they drive down to Pouilly. Miranda stops at Alberti's house (he is her godfather) while Afric drives on to break the news to her mother. Alberti tries to dissuade Miranda, but to no avail. Finally, in desperation, when she has said that times are different and that men are no longer of the romantic generation, he becomes angry and in a stirring speech tells her what he sees as the truth, without sparing her feelings. "Miranda, men don't change. And women are the same. No one at home here has ever told you the truth. Your father has gone God knows where gallivanting after God! Evading his responsibilities. The attractive women get the men" (254). He tells her that the other women work hard to make up for their lack of beauty. They may grow clever and sympathetic, but they must see that men are human beings. He accuses her of giving in to flattery and being praise-hungry. He tells her also that he is tired of hearing about her problem and that out of revenge for her mother he is telling her what he thinks. She isn't worth all the discussion. Perhaps she should go ahead and marry her pansy. At least she would be settled.

Miranda is shaken by this outburst, especially as Alberti has literally turned away from her, and she leaves. The scene that follows at home is another of the highlights of the novel. Lewis Afric has been talking to an angry Ruby when Miranda arrives; James, too, has just joined them, discovering the ring and the occasion. Afric shakes hands with James telling him that Lady Maclean doesn't want Afric to marry her daughter; even so, he and Miranda are determined to be married. " 'Ah, but I'm going to marry her,' said James" (256). He asks Miranda then to marry him and apologizes for doing it in this public way, saying also that he planned to ask her this day but that she was in Paris.

During this interchange one is reminded at first of the dialogue of a Noel Coward play, but the tone becomes more serious:

"You're mad," said Miranda. "We're engaged. I wear his ring."

"Ring, ring!" said James impatiently. "Don't be an idiot, Miranda! It's for life! All our lives, till we're dead. It's for our children, it's for when you're an old woman and I'm an old man. Don't be fatheaded, Miranda. You're a conceited girl besides being a humble one. You've got a habit of pretending you're right even when you know you are in the wrong. You're not right now, you're dead wrong." (256)

He tells her then that he loves her and wants to marry her. He'll look after her until his "bones crumble." In order to save embarrassment, he says, he will go back into the house and wait for her in the library.

For Miranda, this revelation has been of utmost importance. As the scene progresses, Ruby refuses to allow Miranda to make another mistake, and Miranda indicates her uncertainty, finally confessing that she has loved James but thought there was no chance for her. Afric leaves angrily, telling them to send the ring back to Cartier's.

The Voice of the Critics

Most of the reviewers at the time of publication were enthusiastic about *The Loved and Envied,* although the American critics were more complimentary than the English. F. Butcher of the *Chicago Sunday Tribune* (7 January 1951, p. 3) wrote: "If any novelist has ever written more understandingly and more enchantingly about the aged and their long shadows of philosophy than Enid Bagnold has in 'The

Loved and Envied,' I have never read that story. But Enid Bagnold's latest book is no more the typical story about aging and aged men and women, than her delightful 'National Velvet' was a typical story about a horse . . . The aged will probably find it full of poignancy and beauty. The young will find it an amusing—even a satirical picture of the aged and aging."[2] Anthony West in the *New Yorker* (27 January 1951) said: "A very good book . . . what 'The Loved and Envied' does and does extremely well, is create an atmosphere of maturity. . . . There is a description of the loss of emotional contact between a woman [Miranda] and her parents that amounts to a tour de force; it is done with a beautiful economy, in terms of a slow ebbing of intensity that shows up the ordinary *Sturm and Drang* account of the process, done in terms of adolescent rebellion, for the crude personal fantasy it usually is. . . ."[3]

One reviewer was critical of the number of deaths in the novel.[4] In answer to that objection: the novel is skillfully plotted between past and present events, and the deaths occur at varying times but are treated simply, not emphasized. The characters react in different ways: some are threatened, some are not. These varying attitudes toward aging and death are part of the purpose of the book, but there is no preoccupation with the subject. For instance, Rose and Edouard have been speaking of many things when Rose confides to Edouard that she thinks often of death. He replies that she musn't, for death "will come when it comes," and thinking about it will not help. Mustn't she prepare, she wonders. "The Church says so," he replies. "But I'm against it. You'll find all drops into place. No one makes a fuss when they get to the brink" (16–17).

A humorous touch comes in the same conversation when Rose wants him to make a promise, but he knows what she is going to say: She says, "Bury me first. Manage it somehow for me. You know I can't stand loneliness." "All right, Madame Egoiste," he says as he has said before (17). Then he changes the subject.

Chapter Six

Passion for the Theater:
The Early Plays

Wartime Theater

World War II and the blitz raised havoc with the London theaters. Those that remained open specialized in popular fare, mainly musicals, comedies, thrillers, mysteries. Music hall entertainers helped to bolster morale; and in 1940 the government subsidized theater companies that would tour the provinces, also to raise morale. The Old Vic's theater was bombed in 1941, and they too began to tour, reassembling again at the war's end under Laurence Olivier and Ralph Richardson and emerging stronger than ever.

Playwrights that had been popular in the thirties were represented in the forties, especially James Bridie, J. B. Priestley, Noel Coward, Emlyn Williams, and Terence Rattigan. In addition, the plays of George Bernard Shaw, Somerset Maugham, and James Barrie continued to be staged.

On 2 July 1941 Noel Coward's *Blithe Spirit* opened at the Piccadilly Theatre to run for 1,997 performances, the English record, broken later in 1957 by Agatha Christie's *The Mousetrap*. In *Future Indefinite* Noel Coward recalls that 1941 opening night: "The audience socially impeccable from the journalistic point of view and mostly in uniform, had to walk across planks laid over the rubble caused by a recent air raid to see a light comedy about death. They enjoyed it, I am glad to say, and it ran from that sunny summer evening through the remainder of the war and out the other side."[1] A month after that opening *Lottie Dundass* opened in California. This was the first of several Bagnold plays that appeared first in the United States with later openings in London.

Both *Lottie Dundass* (1941) and *Poor Judas* (1946) are plays about artists, and the unrealistic plots are related by theme. Both deal with the frustrations of the artist who cannot follow his art. In *Lottie Dun-*

dass the main character is a would-be actress; in *Poor Judas* he is a would-be writer. Both characters are unpleasant, selfish people, who exploit others and feel themselves justified in doing what is necessary to accomplish their ends. How much does the artist owe to himself? Everything, they say. Talent is the factor that makes all actions forgivable. The two plays were published together in 1951 in a volume called *Theatre*.

Lottie Dundass

When *Lottie Dundass* was produced in Santa Barbara, California, the *New York Times* of 22 August 1941 carried a brief news story of the event:

SANTA BARBARA: The world premiere of "Lottie Dundass" an English murder mystery play by Enid Bagnold was presented tonight (Aug. 21) by David O. Selznick as his second Santa Barbara Summer Theatre play. The attractive young Irish actress, Geraldine Fitzgerald, was starred in the play, which was given before a capacity crowd at the Lobero Theatre. The cast included Dame May Whitty and Joanna Roos . . . Interest in Selznick's treatment of this new play brought out an outpouring of stars, directors and producers from Hollywood. W. Somerset Maugham headed the literary contingent. Pax Walker, young British war refugee, now in Hollywood, was much at home in the piece, as several of the sets represent the Theatre Royal at Brighton, England, and that is where Miss Walker played her first role . . . The play will continue through Sunday.[2]

The London opening came two years later (July 1943) at the Vaudeville Theatre where it ran for five months. In the *Autobiography* Enid Bagnold relates the experience that led to the writing of the play. Maurice Baring, the author, had come to live in Rottingdean some time before the war. He was very ill, and for a period she visited him almost every evening. As she sat reading to him one winter evening, she received a call from the Theatre Royal at Brighton asking that she come in to substitute for the ill Juliet Duff who was to read a Prologue at the opening night of the play *Heil Cinderella*. Cecil Beaton had brought this amateur company as a fund-raiser for a war charity. Bagnold said yes, and she appeared that night in Juliet's somewhat too tight dress. She found the stage experience so exhilarating that she spent most of the rest of the night memorizing the Prologue for the next performance; Juliet, however, came in on the following night though still ill with the measles, and Bagnold in frustration and anger complained to Maurice. He suggested that she write a play about the experience; *Lottie Dundass* was the result.

The play is classified as popular fare: it is serious, yet fanciful, with suspense, ending as a thriller. It begins in a setting that is again the small English village by the sea, like Rottingdean (close to Brighton), as in *National Velvet* and *The Squire*. Only now the time is January with unusually bitter cold and deep snow. Aside from the obvious differences in narrative technique between the novel and the play form, the focus of the story is not within the family or limited to the home locale. The family of a mother with seven children (four at home) is middle class, living in the "Bungalow Colony" on the Downs above the sea.

Lottie Dundass is twenty years old, bright and talented but with sociopathic tendencies. Her one dream, more important than anything else, is to become an actress. The problem is that five years before after an illness she developed a serious heart condition. For a time, apparently, she has been enrolled in a drama school, but the hard work and strenuous hours have been too much and, by doctor's orders, forbidden.

The play opens on a note of mystery and the remnants of a family scandal. Five years before the father, Absalom Dundass, strangled a young actress in the variety show in which he worked as an actor. In the ensuing murder trial he is judged insane and committed to an asylum. Absalom, of little talent himself, has had to live with the image of a famous actor-father whom he hated. Lottie denies her father and worships the image of her dead grandfather whom she has never really known. She wants to be like him. She feels she has greatness and that great people have a right to be selfish.

The plot in brief is that she learns that a touring company (doing one of the many plays she has memorized) is coming to Brighton. It appears then that the leading lady has had an attack of appendicitis and is in the hospital. The understudy, away for the weekend, is snowbound, and the play is to open that Monday night. Lottie's friend Rose is doing temporary secretarial work for the director, and on Monday as they are frantically seeking a solution to the problem, Rose suggests that Lottie fill in, as she knows the part. The idea is not entertained seriously until the director learns that she is the granddaughter of the famous actor, R. S. Franklin. Lottie is over-joyed at the opportunity, and, after meeting the company, she and they go down to the theater to rehearse. No one is particularly thrilled about the idea. She mixes up cues, and they all feel that there is something frightening about her, but she will do. In the mean-time, Eva, the snowbound understudy, has called to say she will try to get an afternoon train but may not arrive on time.

Lottie, dressed and ready to go on that evening, is stunned when Eva arrives. Eva hurriedly prepares her makeup and tells Lottie to get out of her dress. Lottie tries to talk her out of appearing. When this fails, Lottie feels justified in doing what she can to get her big chance. With the belt of the dress she catches Eva unawares and strangles her. She pushes the sofa in front of the body and then per-suades her friend Rose, who has just come in, to sit on the sofa and wait for her as she goes on stage for act 1. Rose has seen nothing and does not know why Lottie is making this strange request.

By the end of act 2, Rose finds the body and understands what has happened. Horrified, she tells Lottie's mother as Mrs. Dundass comes backstage. Lottie asks just to be allowed to finish act 3. In the excite-ment and stress and amid the congratulations from the cast for the fine performance so far, Lottie, displaying increasing signs of insan-ity, has an angina attack. Rose and Mrs. Dundass quickly get the medicine from Lottie's bag, as she slips into unconsciousness. The mother now realizes the agony that is ahead for Lottie, a trial and prison or the asylum; therefore she withholds the amyl nitrate drops. Lottie dies, but the distraught mother feels she has done the right thing for her daughter's sake as well as for her own and the rest of the family.

Mrs. Dundass is a woman of courage and strength, much like Mrs. Brown in *National Velvet*. She has had the task of keeping the family together and living out the disgrace of the children's father. Lottie worships her mother and has told Rose that she doesn't believe in God; "I believe in mother."[3] Mrs. Dundass loves her but feels guilt about Lottie's weaknesses, as though she herself has transmitted a "bad seed." The assumption is that heredity is the most influential factor in forming character and personality.

As far as Lottie is concerned, the father is the symbol of what is bad—not just because he committed murder but because he was in-significant, an actor without talent. The grandfather is the symbol of good because he was a genius, although not a kind person. Lottie believes she has inherited her grandfather's genius, yet fears secretly that she may be more like her father in temperament.

Bagnold creates suspense from the beginning of the play, partly preparing for the violent ending by exposing the signs of Lottie's instability and ruthlessness. One sees her in contrast to the kind and compassionate characters, the normal, good people such as Leppie Dow, the young plumber's helper who is in love with her; Rose, her loyal friend, willing to do whatever Lottie asks, "used" by her; and the mother who sees Lottie's destructive influence on her other children and tries to shield them. Lottie wants all of her mother's attention. In this sense she seems more a child than a young woman; she avoids helping with the children or the housework. In each scene some aspect of the sociopathic personality appears. At the end of act 1, scene 1, she says to her mother: "Oh . . . you an' me. Lovely when the children . . . Don't we wish the children would all . . . fade away?" (*LD, 19*).

In act 1, scene 2, when she is working as a temporary typist for Pratt and John, Builders, she receives phone calls from the people in distress because of the severe cold, those with burst pipes and broken furnaces. She is so occupied with her own dreams that she almost forgets to report the leaking ceiling at the nursery and the burst boiler at school. She is practising a scene from the play *Evelyn Innes,* a dramatization of a novel by George Moore, the play which is to come to Brighton. When the telephone rings with its emergencies, she takes if off the hook and buries it under the cushions of the chair, symbolically stifling the life it represents.

At the end of act 2, scene 1, she shows up at the Albion Hotel in response to the call from Rose. With Mr. Porphory, the producer, she shows confidence, no humility and no fear. Later, an older actress admits that now and then Lottie's voice sounds like her grandfather's.

Despite gradual evidence of Lottie's emotional turmoil, the strangling by the same method her father used five years before, comes as a shock, not altogether prepared for. Lottie's measure of insanity, supposedly, is shown by her lack of conscience, her reveling in the moment and feeling that murder is justified in the satisfaction it has given her in being able to prove that she has her grandfather's talent. She is elated by the experience. In the play within the play the main character has a reconciliation with her father. Lottie practices this scene over and over, but it never moves her to consider a reevaluation of her own father. The irony, of course, is that she has her father's nature and temperament and will suffer punishment because of them. Her glorious debut is also her swan song, and she never gets the chance to finish the last act.

Sybil Thorndike as Mrs. Dundass and Ann Todd as Lottie provided the play with good acting, but the plot remains farfetched. One problem is that we are encouraged to dislike Lottie from the moment she enters. She throws her wet clothes about, is angry with Rose for not waiting in the icy cold at the bus stop, is disagreeable to her mother, and obviously enjoys emphasizing her ailments, lying when she feels the need for attention. The callousness and insensitivity that supposedly are signs of her mental disturbances make it difficult to be sympathetic or to care what happens to her.

Bagnold's forte is her marvelous use of language, but she seldom has the chance to show it in this play. The dialogue is ordinary; it becomes vibrant when Lottie agonizes in frustration over her delicate health. She tells Rose: " . . . If you really knew me you wouldn't like me. I haven't any pity. I haven't any kindness. I'm so angry with the world. If I could find somebody whose fault it was I could mow them down. If it was their fault I could punish . . . But it's here inside me! I'm TOO DELICATE. That's something I can't mow down!" (*LD*, 25).

Later, when she talks about her mother, her pillar of support, one empathizes and may appreciate the metaphor she uses in describing herself: ". . . I came out of mother, I believe she knows me, I believe she's picked me over. I'm her embroidery, I'm her knitting, she knows the stitches and where the dropped ones are and how she's covered them over . . . " (*LD*, 26).

The big question that Lottie wishes to know about her mother but that she is afraid to ask is, "Does she think I'm made of . . . father? Or grandfather?" (*LD*, 26). In the few moments when she reveals her anxieties both she and the language are most effective.

The characters in this play are less real than the people of the novels. Some of the same problems are evident in *Poor Judas*, yet the plays together gain strength in their portrait of the unfortunate artist who cannot succeed, either through his own weaknesses or through lack of opportunity or talent. Not much sympathy is given to either of the main characters, and it may be that Bagnold is showing impatience with the disagreeable, exploitive person who masquerades as an artist, wearing clothes that are too big for him.

Poor Judas

Poor Judas was produced at the Bradford Civic Theatre in November 1946. It is Bagnold's only work utilizing as setting England and France of World War II. Act 1 takes place in France in Dieppe and begins on the evening of the day in 1939 when war was declared. Dieppe is filled with people eager to leave for England. There is already a conflict between the two men working in an upper room, overlooking the sea: one is an elderly Czech scholar named Jules Pasdeloupe Calas and the other is an Englishman, a fifty-two-year-old alcoholic writer named Edward Mission Walker. They have been working together for the past eleven years on a scholarly project which is Calas's lifework. Part of the conflict is caused by Walker's belief that he is too talented a poet to be doing the kind of translating, historical rewriting, and editing that he has been doing.

Mr. Crispin, a publisher, stops by on his way back to England, wanting to get permission to publish an earlier work of Calas. When he sees the monumental project, amounting to ten volumes of manuscript being readied, he is intrigued. Calas at this stage tries to hide the identity of the new work, but Walker tells the publisher what it is: *The History of Herd Treachery*—the history of political wickedness over the years in major countries of the world. The publisher must leave to catch a midnight ship but asks to be contacted regarding the project. Only one to two years' work are left to complete the gigantic task, Calas says; specifically this amounts to two volumes of notes dealing with Poland and England.

One meets also Walker's sixteen-year-old daughter Jenny, neglected by her father, a widower for some years.

In the last scene of act 1, several months have passed and it is now June 1940 at the end of the evacuation of Dunkirk. The Germans are upon them and Walker is hurriedly packing to leave Dieppe for England. Calas is upset that Walker is going, for now he admits that he cannot do without him and is anxious to finish the work. In the confusion and scramble of leaving Walker offers to take the notes of the English section and complete the writing on his own in England. As soon as the war is over or whenever possible, they will get together. Calas, therefore, ties up the bundle of papers and gives them to Walker; almost immediately he regrets letting the notes go.

Act 2 takes place four years later, September 1944, in the English seacoast village of New Haven. The setting is Walker's home where he lives with his now twenty-year-old daughter Jenny and her governess, Virgil Brown. Walker, supposedly, is spending his days working on the project. For four years the household has revolved around the finishing of Calas's project, and they expect that fame and fortune will follow its publication. Walker's ladies cater to his every whim, but one has suspicions that all is not well.

A young Royal Canadian engineer comes for dinner to the obvious delight of Jenny: during a stressful conversation Walker confesses that he has dropped the historical project and is engaged in his own creative work. Just after this damning admission, when Walker has gone from the room, Calas and the publisher, Mr. Crispin, arrive unexpectedly.

As act 3 opens, Walker is missing, and everyone has been waiting for him for several hours. Finally, the agitated Calas asks to see the manuscript which is in the box that no one is allowed to open. Jenny gives permission to pry open the lid since only Walker has a key. They discover then that the box contains notebooks filled with scribblings and that the original bundle of notes is just as it was brought from France years before, still tied up, untouched.

In the emotional crisis that follows Calas has a stroke and when Walker finally appears, everyone is still shaken by the breach of faith, for there is no satisfactory explanation. The angry publisher, with the stricken Calas and their driver, leaves, he stating that he will at least publish the portion of the manuscript brought from France.

From Walker's boastings one assumes that he has finished his own monumental work and that the artist has been true to himself, but then through the questions of the young engineer Smithie it becomes clear that there is no finished work; Walker says that he will now feel free to begin one. During the past four years he has pretended to be working on the book, living a lie, not only in regard to the others, but also to himself. Apparently he has not had the talent or self-discipline to create a meaningful work.

As in *Lottie Dundass,* Bagnold makes her artist disagreeable. There is a sharp contrast between the scholar Calas and the would-be poet Walker. Calas has dedicated his life to his work. His physical needs are subordinated to the need to finish the task. Every moment is precious, and he is irritated at the time Walker spends wandering about in the evenings and in the cafes, drinking. Walker is always ready to eat and drink, resentful of the years he has spent on the task though he knows the finished study would be a worthwhile contribution to society.

When Calas hired him, Walker was forty-one, and as Calas reminds him, "Self-indulgent, insignificant, hopeless, beaten. . . Filling garrets with faded poems—with thoughts on life written on cafe-cards . . . I took you, saved you, harnessed you. I set you on your feet. . . . And the feet have grown too big for your boots! Instead of staining little note-books with your personal droppings you have learnt to serve Humanity."[4] The scholar, too, can be brutal, but one can see the contempt he feels for the misdirected or goalless artist of little talent. Besides the money paid him by Calas, Walker wants recognition by being named coauthor; Calas has refused, saying that he will receive acknowledgment on the title page. Walker complains that he has been working eleven years but with no glory. He feels he could have been a poet. The relationship between Calas and Walker has been uneasy, and though Calas is quick to criticize, he recognizes Walker's importance to him.

From the first, however, one can see that Walker is to be an unsympathetic character: he is described as, "fifty-two, fat and gone to seed with a manner much older than his years, a pink-striped seedy shirt, no collar . . . he polishes his nose with a variegated handkerchief" (*PJ,* 94). His manuscript piles are messy while Calas's notes are neat. He is rude to the old woman, Gabba, Calas's servant from the town. He calls her "Sheep's Head!" or "Wicked goose" or "Obstinate fowl!"

What is also damaging to his image is that he seems to be a neglectful parent. Jenny, his daughter, wears a blouse fastened to her skirt with a big safety pin; her clothes are "bought cheaply in Dieppe" (*PJ,* 98). Gabba criticizes the father for his neglect, but he appears helpless in practical matters. "Is it my fault?" he asks while Gabba replies, "Whose else?" (*PJ,* 100). His behavior, too, is uncouth. At one point, as they work, Walker takes out his upper dentures, holding them up before him.

While he and Calas work, the mundane activities are carried on by Gabba and Jenny. They come in as unobtrusively as possible to nail the blackout paper on the windows. Much is happening outside, war activities, to which the men seem to be oblivious. The work of daily living and eating is seen to by the women.

One realizes with surprise, when Walker comes back to England, that all along he has been financially independent. His daughter (at twenty) has a governess, a situation which appears in sharp contrast to her neglected state in the Dieppe years, but even in England she does not get much attention from her father. Since Walker need not work for a living, he is free to pursue his creative urges; his greatest worry at the moment, however, is that during the war his wine supply has become depleted, and as act 2 begins (1944), he has only four bottles of excellent burgundy left and no prospects of getting more from France.

Jenny and her governess, Virgil Brown, as the managers of the household, are completely attuned to Walker's needs and wishes. The big concern is always the important project that he will be finishing soon, and then, they believe, there will be a big change in their lives, for the better. Walker is no more pleasant in his own household, however, than he was in Calas's.

As in *Lottie Dundass,* the minor characters are sympathetic. Jenny is a warm, unsophisticated girl, plain, eager, love-starved; she has always been kept in the background; she believes in her father and tries to please him. At twenty she is anxious for love to come and therefore is happy when Minnie Pigeon invites Smithie to tea; once Jenny and Smithie become friends during this stressful time, they quickly become committed to each other.

Virgil is more overseer of the household than governess. She is overwhelmed by the idea that Walker is a writer and does all possible to see that he receives the attention he deserves. He, on the other hand, is often rude to her. She seems high-minded and is obviously sincere in her regard for Walker, the creative historian; but when she discovers that he has been a fraud and has deluded the true scholar, she is ready to leave the household and goes off to London with Calas and the others.

Enid Bagnold obviously admires the elderly rugged women who are of the common people. One sees this in her treatment of Gabba in Dieppe. These native women have common sense, are honest, warm, outspoken, and protective of the young as Gabba is of the younger Jenny. Minnie Pigeon, an elderly lady from the shacks up on the Downs, who drops in to bring vegetables, is of this sort also. Hers is a wisdom that sees through sham. She invites the Captain (Smithie) for tea, which becomes dinner—for Jenny's sake. Walker is rude to her, saying: "And as for you—don't put your evil spell on my holy room" (the room in which he writes, apart from the house). She has come to say that a light has been left on and that they must prepare for the blackout. She responds to him by indicating her displeasure: "Ah . . . you think you've got a freedom—but I don't like writers. They're for themselves, an' nothing left for others. I like a man that sweats." He shouts at her: "That's all you know! Don't I sweat down in that room of mine! Are not the beads divine!" "Divine indeed!" Minnie snorts . . . "As for that room of yours . . . full of bottles I wouldn't wonder" (*PJ,* 143).

Walker is secretive and doesn't want people investigating or looking at his papers. His special room is carefully locked, as is the box in which he is putting finished manuscripts.

Captain Smith of the Canadian Royal Engineers is a strong character, one whom Enid Bagnold, no doubt, understood well since both her father and brother were Royal Engineers. His description, however, is humorous: he has "a lift of red hair which boils upwards and his face is cherry-red from the sun. Otherwise he is not remarkable" (*PJ,* 135). After the introduction he is referred to as Smithie. He is cheerful and friendly, admitting that he hasn't dined in a private house in months. Walker is annoyed at the interruption and is not responsive. He has discouraged visitors who might disturb his quiet and his creative energies. Jenny is elated and graciously pours a drink for Smith and herself, straight rum to which she is not accustomed. Walker is worried that he might have to share his precious burgundy with the visitor.

Later, when he discovers that Smithie has the soul of a poet and was brought up with a love of literature, he becomes more genial, especially when Smithie admits that he finds writing and abstract thinking difficult because of his active, physically fit life-style. The fact that writing has become almost an impossibility seems to strike a responsive chord in Walker's psyche, and from then on he is willing and eager to share the burgundy with Smithie.

The language is eloquent, if somewhat exaggerated, in the speeches created for Walker in which he describes the frustrations and loneliness of the writer; it is difficult to judge the degree of sincerity; is he making excuses for himself? In answer to Smithie's wish to talk about writing, he says: "What does a writer do on a beautiful day, tell me that! . . . (loud, savagely) He pulls the curtains to! He shuts it out.

He stays in the dark with his sour soul. He immures himself and listens to his limping mind. That's what a writer does! (Gets heavily to his feet in his anger) There are summer days, let me tell you, when the morning stands up like a yellow pillar, and I feel like a boy, and what do I do then? I set off again to that room of mine that smells of failure. And the months and the years crawl on and the book fills, and the man empties" (*PJ*, 140).

Smithie points out that the historian, at least, always has his material: "You don't depend on imagination. When you're in a hole, you've always got some meat to chew on." Walker protests, "Meat to chew on! What meat can I chew on when the word is absent, when the word won't come! I chewed my hands, sir, in despair this morning" (*PJ*, 142). At that point Virgil mentions that Walker's hands (nails) are beautifully cut and polished. Irony is present throughout the play, especially in Walker's speeches and behavior. His lack of credibility becomes more obvious; and when Smithie asks him if he is nearing the end of his history book, he nods, "Nearing . . . nearing the end."

Smithie's response is unexpected. "I don't believe a word of it," he says. Suddenly he is in control and Walker is on the defensive. "I smell a lie. I'm drunk, and sad, and sun struck and frightened of tomorrow, and frightened of how I shall bear myself, and a little mystic" (*PJ*, 145). But he tells Walker that he doesn't fit, that he is concealing something. He asks for the truth.

One sees Smithie as courageous rather than disrespectful. No one has dared to question Walker before. He has been allowed to continue the charade. Walker, perhaps relieved, confesses that he has abandoned the history, but he is not ready to admit the truth; he says proudly that the seed-corn has put out a green shoot in him and that it has blossomed, implying that he has been working on his own masterpiece. This crucial moment comes at the end of the act, just before the dramatic, unexpected appearance of Calas and his publisher.

Act 3 opens with suspense, and the climax comes when Calas orders the driver to pry open the box, and at the bottom is the bundle of manuscript notes tied with the red dressing-gown cord just as it came from Dieppe. It is Calas who first calls Walker a Judas. His part of the project is finished. The others agree that Walker has betrayed Calas. When the publisher Crispin protests that this great work has been left lopsided and wants an explanation of what Walker has done, Walker readily admits his guilt; he has failed Calas, broken his promise, and has done nothing on the project. Then he produces the artist's argument that "every man tries to build his own pyramid . . . It's contrary to nature to want to reform the world. . . ." Later he continues the biblical allusion of the Judas figure when he says, "It's we—the Incorporate, the Gamblers, who sell life for the crown on the brow" (*PJ*, 161). He asks how anyone can know his problems or what private battles he has fought.

He says then that he has finished his own work, his own pyramid, and asks the vital question, "Now . . . the point is . . . was I right?" Crispin answers coldly, "The point is . . . how much talent had you?" But Walker denies that that was ever the question. His talent is a certainty. For a man of his character, he says, the victory is in being finished (*PJ*, 162). No one, however, will accept that argument.

Smithie's reality is very different from Walker's. In a few hours he is to leave for France, to go into battle. Walker's world is a sheltered creation. For a brief moment Walker considers suicide, but death is no answer, he decides. One sees him as cowardly.

At the end of the play Walker is left alone with Jenny and Smithie, and he wants to celebrate the liberation of the artist to do what he has to do. At that point one discovers that he has created nothing yet. Smithie and Jenny regard him "with pity and horror" (Bagnold's description). The Judas figure is to be pitied. He has betrayed himself also. There is no reason to believe that the future will be different.

One problem with the interpretation of Walker and the other characters is that there is no background information. Walker was living the life of a struggling poet when Calas met him, but for how long? How has he spent the first forty-one years of his life?

Walker is aware of Calas's dependence upon him, and in promising to finish his part Walker made a commitment, but Calas knows from experience that Walker is not entirely reliable and is uneasy about parting with the important notes. Only with prodding and insistence has he kept Walker working for over eleven years. Calas has called himself the old leather whip that every artist needs; but once the connection is broken, Walker obviously feels little need to comply with his promise. As it is, he has shaken off the performance but apparently not the guilt. Otherwise, why pretend that he is working on the history? It is as though the historical work is a prestigious undertaking and a respectable way of spending one's time, whereas writing poetry, perhaps, is not. One never discovers what it is that Walker is writing or attempting to write. His behavior is a mystery.

Walker's inability to build his own pyramid may be the result of laziness, lack of confidence, lack of self-discipline or perhaps, most important of all, lack of talent. The artist is forgiven much if he has talent; Walker has not yet admitted lack of talent.

Jenny asks if her father has done a terrible thing, and Smithie answers that he has by the usual standards men rely on, but that every artist betrays somebody and makes promises to life that he can't keep. Walker has staked a lot, Smithie says, but it is on his promise to himself that everything hangs. "It depends on if he's pulled it off whether he's got his hell coming to him" (*PJ,* 163). Lottie Dundass claims that the artist with genius must be selfish and is not governed by rules that others must abide by; Walker has the same philosophy.

Aside from the Judas figure, neither play contains symbolism, but in both plays the belt becomes a significant object. In the earlier play it was the means of murder. In the latter play it was used for the tying up of the precious manuscript notes. Since it is the belt of Calas's red dressing gown, the binding is immediately identifiable. In one sense Walker, too, commits murder since the shock causes Calas to lose his senses and his creative life. His life's work may be published as is, but he will never know that it has been.

Despite the seriousness of much of the play, touches of humor appear throughout. Most of these come in the characterization and in the ironic moments when people are mistaken in their insights. Walker's exaggerations and affectations are amusing. At one point, for example, he is describing to Virgil the difficulties of writing: ". . . Why should *you* know how I fall by the wayside and pick myself up again? How should *you* know with what fear I cease to believe?. . . (working himself up, but reseating himself, glass in hand). The Pharoahs had bricks! I tear my heart out by myself to build my pyramid! (Silence) What have you got for dinner?" (*PJ,* 134). The sublime is toppled by the mundane.

There is humor also in the exaggerated conditioning in the household, as when Smithie and Jenny are setting the table. Suddenly Jenny interrupts their conversation, saying, "Hush . . ." Walker has taken out one of his little notebooks and has had an inspiration. All activity and talk cease while the inspired writer finishes his thought.

As he concludes the scribbling and returns the notebook to his pocket, Jenny explains quietly that they never disturb him until he has recorded the momentary inspiration.

On the whole, *Lottie Dundass* is a better play than *Poor Judas*. It has a more straightforward plot line and is more theatrically effective, but in the latter play Bagnold displays more of her skill with language and wit. *Poor Judas* had a limited engagement of three weeks but received the Arts Theatre Prize in 1951 for a new play of contemporary significance.

Gertie, "The Flop"

After *Poor Judas* came the ill-fated play *Gertie*. In an article entitled "The Flop" in the *Atlantic Monthly* (October 1952) Bagnold speaks with humor of her adventures with the New York production of *Gertie*. As it happened, this was her first air flight to America and she had many fears. She says, ". . . already sick for home in the dark, and with my little talent like a goldfish in my breast, I climbed into the plane."[5] The metaphor of the little goldfish as her talent appears several times in the account.

She speaks kindly, if ironically, of the director, saying that he was a man of experience and integrity, that he did not appreciate criticism and was capable of rage. She says of herself, "I have a face which takes on a mask of rage greater than I feel. So had he. His face would pale and his eyes would color to the shade of maroon in leather. Being bald he wore his hat continually against draft. The pitch of his hat became for me the bathing flag when the sea is rough" (54).

There were difficulties and much rewriting. She rewrote the third act four times and appreciated the willingness of the company to re-learn lines.

The play opened at the Plymouth Theatre on 30 January 1952, a Wednesday, and closed on Saturday. The critics' reactions were negative: she recalls: "My play, they said in effect, was written backwards when it wasn't written sideways. And in any case static. It was the description of a crab frightened at its feast" (57).

All was not lost. At the party following the end of the play she met Irene Mayer Selznick who was to be the producer of her next and most important play, *The Chalk Garden*. Miss Selznick, daughter of

Louis B. Mayer, the noted film producer, was a striking figure, and Enid Bagnold was much impressed.

A few days after the close of the play, she left New York—by ship—lamenting that "the little goldfish had been no traveler"; her talents had not been extensive enough nor her experience.

Gertie, renamed *Little Idiot,* appeared in London the following year in November but with no better success.

Chapter Seven

The Theater: At the Peak with *The Chalk Garden*

Evolution of the Play

When Enid Bagnold sent the first version of *The Chalk Garden* to Harold Freedman in New York, he telephoned her, saying "This play makes it worthwhile my being an agent" (*A*, 288). With *The Chalk Garden* she reaches the peak of her career as a playwright. It is the most successful of her plays and well on the way to becoming a theater classic.

Its potential for success was not apparent to everyone, since several London agents had refused the play, one of them complaining that he did not care for allegories. This response puzzled her, for, she says, she hadn't realized it was an allegory, and perhaps strictly speaking it isn't, but allegorical elements and various symbols appear throughout.

The production became a reality when Irene Mayer Selznick agreed to do the play on Broadway, if she could do it *her* way. This agreement turned into a friendly, sometimes difficult, and certainly productive relationship lasting many months. Irene came to England to work with the playwright, but even from the beginning there were differences, some as basic as to how much emphasis to place on theme. Irene insisted on a central theme evident throughout the play. For Bagnold, working in terms of several themes crisscrossing, appearing, and disappearing, this requirement was frustrating.

In the rewriting ideas were eliminated, pieces of the script put in the wastebasket, and new lines were created. Bagnold humorously describes one major crisis involving a newly written line that suggested that "there was no love in heaven." Irene would not tolerate that idea: "She put the script down on her lap. The carved eyes were level. 'If there isn't love in your imagined heaven,' she said, 'I go back to New York tomorrow' "(*A*, 292).

85

And then fairly late in the evolution of the play in New York, Irene insisted that there had to be a new scene, a special one in the third act, between the judge and Madrigal. It was written but not without opposition. Once the play was finished to the satisfaction of both, Irene Selznick loyally defended the play and the words as written. This was no easy task, for often the actors and even the director felt no reverence for the beautifully crafted lines.

Irene Selznick engaged Gladys Cooper in London for the part of Mrs. St. Maugham, Siobhan McKenna for Madrigal, and Betsy von Furstenburg for Laurel. Bagnold chose Cecil Beaton to design the set. George Cukor, the director, asked Bagnold to do a recording of the play in her own words so that the proper inflections and mood would emerge.

There were problems with the director (Albert Marre replaced George Cukor), problems with the star, Gladys Cooper, and problems with the set; to make matters worse, the out-of-town openings were dismal; but somehow, in the last moment, the magic worked and the play was a huge success. It opened at the Ethel Barrymore Theater on Wednesday, 26 October 1955, and ran for 181 performances, closing on 31 March 1956.

The London production, too, was a success, running for twenty-three months, with John Gielgud directing and Dame Edith Evans as Mrs. St. Maugham. Kenneth Tynan's review in the London *Observer* paid a handsome tribute to the play:

On Wednesday night a wonder happened: The West End Theatre justified its existence. . . . One has thought it an anachronism, wilfully preserving a formal, patrician acting style for which the modern drama has no use, a style as remote from reality as a troop of cavalry in an age of turbo-jets. One was shamefully wrong. On Wednesday night, superbly caparisoned the cavalry went into action and gave a display of theatrical equitation which silenced all grumblers . . .

The occasion of its triumph was Enid Bagnold's *The Chalk Garden* (Haymarket) which may well be the finest artificial comedy to have flowed from an English (as opposed to an Irish) pen since the death of Congreve. . . . We eavesdrop on a group of thoroughbred minds, expressing themselves in speech of an exquisite candour, building ornamental bridges of metaphor, tiptoeing across frail causeways of simile, and vaulting over gorges impassable to the rational soul.[1]

Autobiographical Elements

The setting of the play is a manor house in Sussex, England, in a village which could be Rottingdean, and Bagnold could well have been Mrs. St. Maugham, the grandmother, for these were her surroundings, and she was sixty-six when the play was written. She was by this time an accomplished gardener, which Mrs. St. Maugham, as hard as she tries, is not.

As in several previous works, notably *Serena Blandish* and *The Squire,* the butler is an influential character; and here we have two, one with the title of butler and all the dignity that that entails and the other of lesser credentials, simply a manservant. The difference between them is that of years of training, tradition, dedication, and a particiular view of the butler's role as an art.

In this play Pinkbell, the bona fide butler, is part of the allegorical fabric of the play. Bagnold takes pains in the *Autobiography* to point out that their butler Cutmore is the prototype of Pinkbell with, of course, some changes. Cutmore, she explains, had been with the family for twenty-nine years. He was proud of his empire, the butler of butlers, emperor of the servant era, but it was a world that was already crumbling by the time he came to work for the Joneses. She speaks of him as being a handsome, though gloomy man with a basic contempt for women. He sometimes accompanied Roderick Jones on his travels, but Jones complained that Cutmore with his height, good looks, and gravity was always mistaken for the Head of Reuters. The butler whom Bagnold created turns out to be rather different from his prototype. Pinkbell is a more ominous figure, despite his frivolous name which reminds one of Tinkerbell in *Peter Pan.*

Sequence of Events

As the play opens, Mrs. St. Maugham has advertised for a companion for her granddaughter, Laurel. By default, so to speak, Miss Madrigal is hired, but there is something strange about Miss Madrigal. On the other hand, sixteen-year-old Laurel is strange too. She has been living with her grandmother for four years since her mother remarried. Maitland, the lesser butler, is a prominent member of the household; more important, but unseen, is Mr. Pinkbell, head butler, in bed upstairs with a stroke. Olivia, Laurel's mother, comes to reclaim her daughter but is opposed by Mrs. St. Maugham. During a luncheon visit of a judge, a friend of Mrs. St. Maugham, one learns that Miss Madrigal has been tried for murder and has been in prison for fifteen years. This is her first experience after her release. The positive influence of Miss Madrigal is so strong, however, that Laurel is persuaded to leave with her mother; and Maitland, also under her spell, would gladly serve her wherever she chooses to go. The play ends as Mrs. St. Maugham is reconciled to Miss Madrigal and the two plan to make the most of their chalk garden and, presumably, the remainder of their lives.

Eccentric Characters

The play does not pretend to be realistic, and the characters may not be in step with ordinary people. They are an imaginative, upper-class group in a special corner of the world. Perhaps one shouldn't be surprised then to find that Laurel, though sixteen years old, is called a "child," is treated like a child, and does indeed behave like a twelve-year-old. While Mrs. St. Maugham is interviewing Miss Madrigal, wild screams are heard from the direction of the garden. Maitland rushes outside, and Mrs. St. Maugham explains that it is her daughter's child, her granddaughter, and that she is fond of screaming. She is, apparently, also fond of setting bonfires and is not to be left alone. When later her mother Olivia comes, again screaming is heard, and when Olivia asks if something is the matter, Miss Madrigal explains that nothing is wrong; Laurel is simply dancing around the bonfire with Maitland.

Laurel also has a talent for exaggeration. She tells the applicants for governess that her grandmother has had a hundred and seven answers when there were only five. She also says that her father shot himself when she was twelve years old and that she was in the room. Then turning to Madrigal as though there were nothing unusual in what she has just said, she asks, "And what are your qualifications?"[2] Actually, Laurel's father died of liver problems when she was three. How much of her behavior is generated in a spirit of fun and how much is need for attention is not clear; but she reminds one of the young girl in Saki's "The Open Window" who confronts the guest with the preposterous story of the "ghostly" hunters and is delighted as the visitor retreats, horrified, when they suddenly appear.

Laurel tries to bully Madrigal, but Madrigal is herself a grown-up version of Laurel, older now and wiser, having suffered through the years and understanding the desperate need to be identified and loved; therefore, Madrigal keeps the upper hand. She sees also the loveless-ness of Laurel's life and would like to save her from herself and from her grandmother.

When Madrigal asks Laurel about her grandmother, "Does she love you?" Laurel answers, "She would *like* to! She *thinks* she does! . . . But I am only her remorse" (42). Laurel has convinced herself that her mother does not love her either and has abandoned her. She also perpetuates the story of a sexual attack in the park on the night of her mother's second marriage, when she was twelve years old.

Maitland, the manservant, is like a big brother to Laurel. It has been his responsibility to look after her and keep her safe. He, too, has spent time in prison, five years as a conscientious objector (during wartime no doubt), and now both he and Laurel have a fascination for courts, trials, and criminal cases. The mystery surrounding Madrigal intrigues them, but they instinctively respect her, and Laurel allows herself to be governed.

Laurel's grandmother is imperious, confident, proud of belonging to the upper class; she says in explaining Laurel's behavior: "Words leap and change color in her mouth like fishes!" She says of her own influence on her granddaughter, "You will note how light my finger lies upon her! The child's a flower. She grows in liberty." Madrigal, however, thinks otherwise: "Weeds grow as easily," she says (32–33). The metaphor of plants for people occurs throughout the play, and in this case Laurel needs discipline or "shaping" and "pruning" if one wishes to extend the metaphor. Laurel understands how to handle her grandmother and knows what pleases her. She tells Madrigal that if she wishes to get along with her grandmother, she must take note of her eccentricity. Mrs. St. Maugham enjoys being imaginative, appar-ently, and also likes to tell creative tales.

Because of the originality and wit of Mrs. St. Maugham's re-sponses, one tends to forgive or at least overlook her cruelty in deal-ing with her daughter Olivia and her not telling Laurel that her mother has written often, has been to see her, and wants to take her home. Olivia, too, has been an unloved child and still bears the brunt of criticism. Her one success, a rich husband, was the marriage Mrs. St. Maugham arranged. Olivia's second marriage, for which her

mother has not forgiven her, is a love match to an army colonel. This
has been a bitter disappointment to Mrs. St. Maugham in the same
way that Olivia herself is a disappointment. She says with distaste,
"Who would have thought you would have taken on that look—so
quickly—of the Colonel's Lady!" (53). Later she wonders if Olivia has
worn the scarf she has on simply to annoy her mother. She takes
Olivia's supposed lapses of taste as a personal affront. She evidently
had great plans for Olivia to figure prominently in the social world
in which Olivia has no interest. Even now she reminds her daughter
that she had to force her into beauty and that even at her wedding
Olivia wore her dress as if it were wrapping paper, also that she was
ever plain, shy, and stubbornly quiet.

Now Olivia is pregnant and Mrs. St. Maugham holds over her
head the fact that Laurel will have a rival in the baby and so will not
receive the care and love she needs. The grandmother has not tried to
discourage Laurel's mistaken notions and hostility to her mother.

Olivia pleads with her mother to forget their past differences and
for once to be on her side. She wants acceptance and help in order to
take Laurel back; it is only through Madrigal's intervention that she
is able to do this. Because Laurel trusts Madrigal's judgment, she is
willing to believe that her mother indeed loves and wants her.

Madrigal continues to be a mystery to the end of the play even
though she has been willing to reveal the secret of her past to save
Laurel from remaining in the arid atmosphere of her grandmother's
house.

Symbolism and Allegory

The allegorical elements of the play deal with the character of Miss
Madrigal, but the allegory is a delicate matter and must be taken
lightly. Miss Madrigal is a bit like Strindberg's Eleanora in the play
Easter. She has mystical qualities and is of a saintly mode with a sensitivity beyond the ordinary, and she seems to "know" things that
are not knowable. Part of this awareness is the result of solitude and
suffering.

Near the beginning of the play she says of one of the candidates for
the position of governess (whom Madrigal has just met) that she is
light-fingered, but not seriously so, one who would take no more
than a box of matches. When Maitland asks if she knows the woman,
Madrigal says no but that she has seen hands like hers many times

before. Her prison experience has allowed her to know many types of undesirable people, but even so, there is a mystic quality in everything she says and does.

She has also an uncanny knowledge of growing plants and an appreciation of the starkness of the chalk garden. Throughout the play the symbol of the chalk garden reappears in relation to an environment lacking love or sufficiently healthy soil for the growth of normal plants or people.

Very soon in the play she becomes the adversary of Pinkbell, the old, forbidding, and terrifying butler whose power is felt throughout the household and who gives orders from his sickbed, but his directives for the chalk garden result in the death of the plants. Madrigal feels that there must be some mistake, for who, she asks, has tried to grow rhododendrons in a chalk garden? Mrs. St. Maugham admits that the plants were put in last autumn and that "they're unhappy!" Madrigal exclaims, "They are *dying*. They are in pure lime. . . . *Nothing in the world has been done for them!*" (59). Plants are like people and must be treated with respect and care. She is horrified at the destruction caused by carelessness and lack of knowledge. This, too, accounts for her concern for Laurel's "weedlike" growth.

Mrs. St. Maugham explains then about Pinkbell, her butler for forty years. He has had a stroke but still retains control over household matters; his standards are the rule of the house. When Madrigal comments that she must be fond of him, Mrs. St. Maugham says no. He has also been training Maitland, but now Maitland will have nothing to do with him. Maitland says later, "I won't take orders from the old bastard!" (26). Laurel uses the same expression when she says that "the old bastard Mr. Pinkbell" was the one who told her to put salt on the fire to turn the flame blue (31).

Pinkbell is an ominous figure for several reasons: one is that he is never seen; also the characters talk about him, call him names, and are obviously in awe of him; he has ruled the household, but orders and pronouncements come to the audience at second hand and are responsible often for the death of the flowers in the chalk garden. Therefore, he assumes an aura of evil. His death, too, is timed or seems to coincide with Madrigal's victory and triumph as a force of good and a proponent of life.

The symbol of the garden, present throughout the play, sometimes merges with the good versus evil theme, and one sees Madrigal as attuned to the knowledge of a higher power. There are numerous references to heaven and God in connection with Madrigal. When the judge asks Mrs. St. Maugham how she discovered Madrigal, she replies that she advertised. She took a chance and has been justified in that choice. She says, "Miss Madrigal came to me like rain from heaven" (129).

When she knows that the judge has recognized her, Madrigal realizes that he may not consider her appropriate for the governess position. She admits that she has private means but finds this a job particularly suited to her. She asks him, "Do you believe in God? I thought God had given it to me!" (130).

Olivia has quickly sensed Madrigal's power for good and, thinking of Laurel, has said to her, "Don't go! The wind blows from the sea here and growing things need protection!" (60).

At the end of act 1, when Madrigal reports that there is a black spot on the roses, Mrs. St. Maugham exclaims, "The *roses!* What would you have done for them! Pinkbell ordered . . . and I *sprayed* them!" Madrigal answers, "With what, I wonder! You had better *prayed* for them!" (61).

Later, Mrs. St. Maugham, the unbeliever, is distraught as she gathers up the broken madonna lilies "Oh—when things are killed in my garden it upsets me—as when I read in the newspapers that my friends die!" (46). During the course of the play Mrs. St. Maugham makes several callous comments; if she means them literally, and it appears that she does, they are inconsistent with her sensitivity about the love and death of flowers.

Laurel seems surprised at her grandmother's reaction to death. She has thought that one found death more natural and less a threat as one grew older. Mrs. St. Maugham dispels that notion immediately. She finds nothing natural about death. In fact, she sees the world as a park in which capricious gods go "rook-shooting" as one walks confidently by. One of the stray shots may be for her. Mrs. St. Maugham sees the universe as haphazard, unfeeling, destructive, with no God in control. Madrigal, on the other hand, knows that one can learn from suffering and exposure to death. She tells Mrs. St. Maugham that a garden is a good lesson, for so much dies in it.

Near the end of the play when Madrigal insists that Laurel go with her mother, Mrs. St. Maugham says, "This girl of special soil! Transplant her?" Madrigal answers, "You have not a green thumb, Mrs. St. Maugham, with a plant or a girl. This is a house where nothing good can be made of her!" . . . "Why even your garden is demented" (144).

The battle between Madrigal and Pinkbell continues. As Laurel and Maitland are discussing the positive influence of the Boss (as she calls Madrigal), Maitland points out that Laurel is the better for her influence, but Laurel says that Mr. Pinkbell doesn't agree; Maitland calls him poison and can see trouble coming. When Laurel reports that Pinkbell is sulking, she adds, "He is full of jealous rage about his Enemy" (73). Madrigal has called him "the devil in charge" (69).

After Madrigal calmly corrects Pinkbell on the telephone, Mrs. St. Maugham reports that her ears are filled with poison. The nurse upstairs says that the old man is crying with rage! Madrigal then tells her that she must choose between them. The elderly lady admits having always been afraid of Pinkbell, and Laurel reminds her that if they want to keep Madrigal, they will have to fight for her. The crisis passes when the judge arrives.

In the last act, after Madrigal seems to have won and Laurel is to leave, the nurse announces that Pinkbell is dead. It is as if an evil force is letting go and quietly slipping away, but Enid Bagnold does not emphasize the evil nor has the fear of Pinkbell ever seemed an overwhelming fear. The touch is light.

There is suspense in the luncheon scene when it becomes clear to the audience that this is the judge that passed sentence on Madrigal fifteen years before. No one else knows. When the judge recognizes Madrigal finally, he is ill at ease and would like to evade the responsibility of identifying her. In this quiet encounter, a beautifully written scene, he admits not knowing what he will do. The tension is almost more than Madrigal can bear; she tells the judge that she can't wait for seven hours again as she did years before. She was sentenced to death on a Tuesday, but that decision was changed. She has already served time, a lifetime to her. She wonders what he can do to her now. He does not presume to judge her twice, he says, but she believes he would come to the same conclusion. Cleverer minds than hers could not convince him. She has learned that innocence is not enough and that added talking gains nothing. She comes of a stock, she says, that cannot accept defeat. The judge says, "You have greatly changed," to which she replies, "At our last meeting I died. It alters the appearance" (133).

Laurel suspects the truth after the luncheon, partly because of Madrigal's strange behavior. For Laurel's sake, then, Madrigal admits to Mrs. St. Maugham that she was the person sentenced to death by the judge, for the murder of her stepsister presumably, although she does not say that. In the shock of this discovery, Mrs. St. Maugham wonders how she can be living then at all, and the judge admits that there was a doubt as to her guilt as the sentence was bypassed.

During their private talk the judge, who has known her as Connie Dolly Wallis, asks about the name "Madrigal." He realizes that she has had to choose another name. "It's more than a name to me," she says (132). Perhaps the name Madrigal calls to mind a joyous song or a folk hymn. Whatever its meaning, she feels apparently that the name suits her and expresses her gratitude at being among the living. She will go on exploring the "astonishment of living" she tells the judge when he asks what she will do (157).

Even though Mrs. St. Maugham is angry with Madrigal, she too senses her uniqueness. She wonders if Madrigal, who seems to have an answer to everything, can tell her if there is an afterlife? "Certainly," Madrigal answers, and when Mrs. St. Maugham seems surprised, she says, "One does not sit alone for fifteen years without coming to conclusions" (162). The elderly lady then asks if there is affection in that world. Madrigal points out that Mrs. St. Maugham has been living all this while without affection. Hasn't she noticed?

Now with Laurel and Olivia gone, Mrs. St. Maugham wonders if she is to die unloved? Madrigal replies, "If necessary. I was prepared to do it" (164). The mystery of Madrigal is not resolved, but Mrs. St. Maugham feels compelled to ask if Madrigal is guilty. In reply, Madrigal wonders why she should know what learned men could not discover in the nine days of the trial. That apparently settles the question as they prepare to work together on the chalk garden.

Diction

In the sparkling words, the humor, and the aphorisms one is reminded especially of Oscar Wilde and George Bernard Shaw. The surface energy and wit give a comedic glow which often belies the seriousness of what happens in the play.

In her *Autobiography* Enid Bagnold stresses the need to recognize the levels of meaning and the nuances in the dialogue of her plays. She points out that the words have to be heard and that the humor depends on an awareness of two levels of meaning, the surface fact and the essence beneath it. The same technique of dialogue is present in all of her plays, but she maintains that only Irene Selznick seems to have brought out these distinctions satisfactorily.

As mentioned previously, many of her lines are aphorisms. For instance, Madrigal says, "The dangerous thing about hate is that it seems so reasonable" (43). When Laurel and Madrigal are speaking, Laurel says, "Are you talking of *you?* Or of *Me!*" Madrigal answers, "When one feels strongly—it is always of *me!*" (44). Mrs. St. Maugham says: "Irritation is like a rash on the heart" (23). And when she says, "Privilege and power make selfish people—but gay ones," this might be Enid Bagnold speaking (23). Maitland says, "Praise is the only thing that brings to life again a man that's been destroyed" (30). Madrigal: "It takes the pity of God to get to the bottom of things" (117).

Sometimes contrary ideas are compressed within one statement as when Laurel says about her grandmother, "She is a great gardener, but nothing grows for her" (7). One of the highlights is the judge's description of the mysterious woman defendant, the Madrigal of fifteen years ago. He repeats the defendant's words: "What I have been listening to in court, she said, is not my life. It is the shape and shadow of my life. With the accidents of truth taken out of it" (120).

In the classic essay on *The Chalk Garden* ("The Madrigal in the Garden," *Tulane Review,* December 1958), Gerald Weales says about the speeches, "In a way, the dialogue suggests Chekhov. The characters speak first of all to themselves and out of themselves; if occasionally they communicate, if their speeches sometimes land on listening ears, the effect is a lucky accident."[3]

This observation seems valid often in this play and in several of Enid Bagnold's plays, but the key word is "suggests" Chekhov. There are major differences otherwise between the two authors in the style and essence of their characters' talk.

Other Productions

The London production of *The Chalk Garden* opened in 1956, the same year in which Bertolt Brecht's Berliner ensemble came to London and a year after Samuel Beckett's startling production of *Waiting for Godot,* directed by Peter Hall. Important changes in theater were to come, and perhaps most significant in determining the direction of drama for the next generation was John Osborne's *Look Back in Anger,* which also opened in 1956. The world of *The Chalk Garden* was disappearing from theater and was being replaced by a world of angry young men, plays with working-class characters, realistic language, and antiestablishment subjects.

One of the most recent productions of *The Chalk Garden* emerged in the spring and early summer of 1982 in New York. It was an artistic triumph with Irene Worth as Miss Madrigal and Constance Cummings as Mrs. St. Maugham. One reviewer commented that the play represents a fusion of "two sturdy British breeds, the drawing room comedy and the detective story."[4]

Actually, the play is not easy to classify. It is partly drawing room comedy without the purpose of a true comedy, without emphasis on romance and without emphasis on the humor; a detective story in which no one knows if there was a crime, a mystery story which is never wholly resolved, an allegory so carefully controlled that many theatergoers are never aware that such elements exist. The result seems a beautifully integrated hybrid in a class of its own.

Jack Kroll, the reviewer of the New York production (1982), also commented on the playwright's style. He said, "As a stylist Bagnold had the greenest of thumbs; she brought forth flowers of wit from the roots sunk deep into meaning. *The Chalk Garden* is very likely the most grown-up, sophisticated, brightly bejeweled play in New York."[5]

The Chalk Garden became a British film in 1964 starring Hayley Mills as Laurel, Deborah Kerr as Madrigal, and Edith Evans as the grandmother. Enid Bagnold had never wanted to adapt her own works into movies, and in an interview with journalist Keith Harper (*Guardian,* 20 August 1965) she gives one reason why: "I asked H. G. Wells when he returned from Hollywood after doing *The Invisible Man* if I should try film writing and he replied: 'I am a tough man and I can do nothing with them. So if I were you I shouldn't try.' "[6]

Chapter Eight

The Later Plays: Limited Success

The three plays discussed in this chapter were produced in the 1960s: *The Last Joke* (1960), *The Chinese Prime Minister* (1964), and *Call Me Jacky* (1968), the same decade in which many of Harold Pinter's important plays, the "comedies of menace," appeared. Pinter was one of Bagnold's favorite playwrights.

The three Bagnold plays have certain features in common: settings in wealthy London homes; eccentric characters, and unrealistic plots. The play that seemed at first to have the most promise, *The Last Joke,* fared the worst in production.

The Last Joke

Originally called *At the Top of His Form, The Last Joke* had personal ties stemming from an important period in Enid Bagnold's life. It was again that exciting time in which she was attending Catherine d'Erlanger's parties in the pre-World War I years and extending through the war, this period when she was living at home at Warren Wood after the London adventure.

She had met Prince Antoine Bibesco, first secretary of the Roumanian Legation. He was rich, handsome, and intellectually stimulating. They fell in love and although the admitted affair did not last long, their friendship endured until his death; in his later years he came often to visit the Joneses in Rottingdean.

Antoine, like Hugo in *The Last Joke,* had a brother who had had a stroke and kept himself apart from the people he had known formerly. Emmanuel wore a blue scarf over the lower part of his face although the marks of the stroke were slight. Antoine tried desperately to please him, as Hugo does with Ferdinand in the play.

On her first visit to Bibesco's London home overlooking the Thames, Bagnold had just come in when to her surprise she saw a door opening and "a hand came through holding out a bunch of wet, dying flowers. 'Take them!' said Antoine in low urgency, his face changing (A, 157). She took them and the door shut. This incident occurs also in act 1 of *The Last Joke* when Rose comes to Hugo's home.

Antoine's brother Emmanuel gradually became a friend to Enid Bagnold, or as much of a friend as he could be in his eccentricity, which included rages and several suicide attempts. Antoine was devoted to his brother and tried to keep him amused; apparently her lively personality suited them both.

Often they sent books to her that they felt she should read. They greatly admired Proust, but somehow she was not considered "eligible" yet for Proust; she claims that they were educating her in a more basic level of French literature. She recognized later that many of their allusions and catchwords were expressions from Proust.

Both Antoine and Emmanuel would telephone her at home, which caused a problem since the telephone was in the dining room, and her father objected to being disturbed at dinner. Emmanuel was perverse enough to delight in doing what was forbidden, and he delighted in ringing at mealtime. One Sunday during lunch Emmanuel called and in the confusion between her father's disapproval and Emmanuel's terse comments, she said she would ring back. Almost immediately she feared that something serious was happening. She tried to ring back, but there was no answer. She telephoned Antoine in London, and he surmised immediately that Emmanuel had committed suicide. She left for London as Antoine had asked her to do. This time Emmanuel had succeeded; he had taken poison and then hanged himself. Antoine was devastated.

He made her promise never to discuss the incident, and she maintained the silence, but forty-five years later, after Antoine's death, she wrote the play that was based on the characters of Antoine and Emmanuel and the suicide. The play's failure, she would say humorously, was Antoine's revenge. He had come back to put a jinx on it.

The original play, she claims, the play that the producer and director believed would be a certain success, turned out to be quite different in the final version, after rewriting especially of the third act.

The Last Joke takes place in Chiswick Mall in the present and it is summer. The set for act 1, the drawing room of the home of Prince Hugo Cavanati, is much like Bagnold's description of Antoine's house overlooking the Thames at 114 Grosvenor Road, with its river-tones of silver and gray Japanese wallpaper and the collection of French Impressionist paintings. In the play an important feature of the set is the photograph of a painting of a woman in a garden by the painter Edouard Vuillard. The picture is of Hugo and Ferdinand's mother, whom they both adored. At one point Ferdinand says (what Antoine had said on the death of Emmanuel), "I have had only two loves! My mother and my brother. . . ."[1]

As the play opens, nineteen-year-old Rose Portal has been attending a small gathering at Hugo's home. Accompanying her is an elderly former diplomat, Baron Santa Clara, called Old Toni, now working for her father. Enid Bagnold's descriptions of characters in her plays sometimes contain metaphors as lively as those of her prose. Old Toni is said to have the "powdery elegance of an old dried fern" (*LJ*, 88). He has known Princes Hugo and Ferdinand in a diplomatic post in Constantinople and at their home in Roumania. He admires Hugo's paintings and then speaks in glowing terms of the absent diplomat brother Ferdinand, of his brilliance as a mathematician and his passion for living. At this point the particular photograph of the Vuillard painting is singled out for attention. The original, Hugo explains, had been stolen twenty years before.

It turns out that Ferdinand has secretly been living here with his brother, avoiding people because of a stroke. Rose discovers this on a surprise return visit. He causes Hugo great anxiety by constant threat of suicide, and Hugo, devoted to his brother, has managed to forestall further attempts by threatening to die also if Ferdinand kills himself.

Ferdinand as the gifted mathematician some time before developed a formula that may explain the essence of God; he has an overwhelming curiosity to seek the other side of life to find if his calculations will prove true; therefore, dying now, he says, is not a rejection of life so much as a discovery of the secrets of another world, confirming the truth of his speculations.

Rose bargains with him when she discovers his interest in the painting. If Ferdinand will urge Hugo to come to the elaborate coming-out ball her wealthy art-collector father is giving, she will tell him where she has seen the painting. Ferdinand surmises correctly that the painting is in Edward Portal's collection. The picture is hidden in his bedroom behind another painting, Rose admits, but it was purchased, not stolen. With delight, considering the humor of the situation, Ferdinand determines that he will visit her father disguised as a Turkish art dealer and pretend to sell him the same painting. Both Hugo and he, therefore, will be guests during the ball. This will be his last joke, he says. Rose is concerned only with getting Hugo to fall in love with her.

Act 2 takes place on the evening of the ball in the library of Wood Castle, rented for the year by Portal. His hobby is art collecting but apparently he has gained his fortune from Arabian oil interests. He has just returned from the Continent. One also meets Mrs. Webster, his lady valet for many years. Ferdinand appears in disguise as Benzuto and is enjoying his negotiations with Portal. Ferdinand's elderly servant Matthew recognizes Portal as the son of the man who was valuing the art objects in Roumania when the painting was stolen. When the identification is definite, Ferdinand instructs Matthew to set off the burglar alarm by pretending to steal an art object. When Portal leaves to investigate, Ferdinand recovers the family painting and leaves through the garden with directions from Rose. When Portal realizes what has happened and who Ferdinand really is, he goes in pursuit, and Rose follows, determined to warn the prince.

Act 3 takes place in a clearing in the woods not far from the house where tables are to be set up for the breakfast after the ball. Ferdinand is seated casually, waiting, as Rose hurries in. He persuades her to go along with his plans, indicating that he approves of her love for his brother and the need to keep Hugo from harming himself. Both he and Hugo have guns. Portal arrives, then Mrs. Webster, to oversee the breakfast arrangements.

In the emotional scene that follows Mrs. Webster reveals that Portal killed his father years before and that she is Rose's mother. It was he, Portal admits, at age sixteen, who stole the painting and then accidentally killed his father in the quarrel that followed. Rose is shaken; however, there is no reconciliation attempt with her new-found mother.

Ferdinand has contrived to take poison, in tablets slipped to him by Matthew, and as Hugo arrives, he gives up his gun as a show of good faith; Hugo gives up his also. Then Ferdinand drinks water from a golden bowl and collapses. After the initial shock, Hugo realizes that he has been freed, by his brother's intention, from taking his own life; and although not yet ready to deal with love, he asks to marry Rose.

The character of Ferdinand dominates the play. From the beginning the baron, called Old Toni, gives him an elaborate buildup of superlatives. The stage directions say that he has ceased to take care of his appearance but that the effects of the stroke are hardly noticeable. His dynamic qualities, however, are emphasized. He is the only character (aside from Edward Portal) described at length. For Hugo there is no description at all and for Rose, only what she wears. About Ferdinand, the playwright says: "he is a passionate, impatient, tyrannical, and charming man; shaken with the gaiety of inscrutable jokes—or with unheralded furies. When he speaks it is with a gusty energy, vigorous, imperious. His gestures are clumsy and violent and objects break that do not obey his will" (*LJ*, 95–96).

He is to be, therefore, a colorful and complex character, and that he is. He manipulates Hugo and the others, behaving sometimes like a spoiled child, keeping his will with him and making revisions periodically. Much of this behavior is humorous, since he enjoys teasing Hugo. He asks, "Am I a sadist?" and Hugo answers, "You crack your death like a whip over my head" (*LJ*, 100).

He is, no doubt, angry at having to curtail his active life because of the stroke, although at present few ill effects remain. He is not an invalid. He is fascinated by the mathematical calculations that may explain God. On the night of his stroke he was explaining his sums to Hugo and talked him to sleep; it was four in the morning, supposedly, when the attack came. Ferdinand says that it was God's punishment, "He struck the gong for my disintegration," the penalty for daring too much.

Ferdinand's lines are witty and delivered with style and arrogance. He relishes the role of Benzuto, the Turkish art dealer, and the baiting of Edward Portal. He shows his knowledge of art and conducts himself with a superiority that makes Portal suspicious, especially since he deliberately makes some outrageously false statements. Benzuto, as he begins to talk of the painting he will offer to Portal, picks up a golden skull:

> PORTAL: *(delighted he shows interest)* My gold skull!
>
> BENZUTO: Soapstone, Gilded.
>
> PORTAL: *(not offended by this; sure of himself)* Tomb Seven! Mount Alban. Oakaca. Xipe Totec. The Flayed God.
>
> BENZUTO: Devastatingly non-survival . . . Used for Black Magic.
>
> PORTAL: Very probably. The Mixtec Death Culture—A.D. Nine hundred.

BENZUTO: *(laying it back on the table)* Nineteen hundred. It belongs to
            Aleister Crowley.
PORTAL: *(Outraged)* Prove it!
BENZUTO: *(Smooth)* A mark on the base.

                                                            (*LJ*, 130–31)

Portal, now angry, asks the others to leave the room before he asks
Benzuto, "Why the charade? . . . Of knowing everything!" Benzuto
answers calmly, "Self-flattery. Warmth. Before risking . . ." As soon
as he can, Portal asks, "Who are you?" but gets no answer (*LJ*, 131).
A bit later when Portal has left the room, Matthew has recognized
him as "Kutz's boy"; he says, "Kutz—he was called. The name's
come back—seeing him. (Impatiently) The *valuer!* That time the picture went—he brought this lad with him!" (*LJ*, 136). He tells Ferdinand to see if the tip of a finger on Portal's left hand is missing. That
will make the identification positive. When Ferdinand discovers that
it is so, they contrive to set off the alarm and then steal the painting.
    Even though he has the painting in his possession, the pursuit of
which took all of act 2, Ferdinand, now seated (act 3), waiting for
the others, is concerned only with staging his suicide. He goads Mrs.
Webster and finally, Portal, into confessing the truth about themselves, and with the help of Rose is able to trick Hugo into giving
up his gun; then without the others being aware, he takes the poison.
He enjoys the drama of the setting, the audience, and the emulation
of Socrates as he sips from the golden bowl.
    Hugo is a much less interesting character than Ferdinand and much
more passive. As the younger brother, he is overshadowed by Ferdinand, apparently, but in the play his role is to react rather than initi-
ate action. He is a foil for his brother; his main purpose is to contain
Ferdinand, to keep him amused and alive. He is so emotionally involved in that mission that he cannot or will not think of love or pursuing his relationship with Rose, even though he admits he might
love her. While she does the pursuing, he does little to encourage or
attract her.
    He is not a part of the attempt to recover the picture, nor in on
the discovery of Portal's identity, and even though Ferdinand has told
him about the mathematical formula, he has little interest in pursuing shadows. He is willing to believe that his brother is right. He is
a good, likable, sympathetic person, worshipping Ferdinand and
ready to give up his life for him. He lacks his brother's arrogance,

preferring not to use his title in England, an attitude that infuriates
Ferdinand.

At the end of the play Hugo is still being obedient when he listens
to the last message from his brother. Ferdinand's servant Matthew
says, *"You are free, Mr. Hugo."* He was to tell Hugo that and that he
was to ask for Rose in marriage. Hugo proposes to her in a wooden,
preoccupied way, which prompts Portal to say to Rose, "He doesn't
love you." Hugo's response and the last words of the play are, "You
can't ask a man you've pulled out of a lake if he loves.
"First. . . (Exhausted) You've got to dry him" (*LJ*, 164).

Rose is radiant and willing to take the responsibility. She is a
strong character, aggressive, sometimes abrasive, and insensitive,
confused, thirsting for love. She is not close to her father, and he admits that he does not understand her, but he tries. He says, "If Rose
were a book—I should say I was illiterate!" (*LJ*, 142). As an art col-
lector, he travels over the world, and Rose now after the convent days
at nineteen is often left waiting in hotels for her father to return from
trips abroad. They have spent considerable time in Paris and have
been in England only a year. She has no companions or confidantes
until Old Toni gives her advice about worldly matters. She is realistic
and understands that, though rich, they do not belong. Toni has arranged the elaborate ball at Wood Castle, purposely obtained by her
father for her coming-out party. Rose tells Hugo, "Toni arranges everything—He says all London's coming!. . . *We* don't know anybody. *We* can't ask anybody. We've only just set up shop as
Pretenders! If you're rich, Toni says, You can always buy your way
in!". . . She is aware also of her father's lack of taste in decorating.
She says, ". . . Come and see what we've made of Wood Castle! It's
hideous" (*LJ*, 92).

Mrs. Webster has shown no warmth, love, or even interest in
Rose, but part of this may have been from a promise of secrecy made
to Portal. Rose, then, has no affection for Mrs. Webster, rather more
often annoyance. She is shocked, therefore, to find out who Mrs.
Webster is. Whenever Rose asked for information about her mother
before, Portal refused to tell her. She wonders at one point if he is
her father.

As in other works, one sees the author's fondness for concise and
witty utterances. Rose asks Ferdinand on their first meeting what he
wants to know about her—what would make her suitable for Hugo.
Ferdinand says, "The depths of your heart—and the length of your

constancy. What do you want—in a man?" Rose answers, "That he should know his way round—at the top of my mind." "And the bottom of your heart?" he asks. She says, "That's not so important" (*LJ*, 109). In the interchange of dialogue one occasionally hears echoes of George Bernard Shaw and sometimes Oscar Wilde.

Edward Portal is another strong character, the villain of the piece, suffering more at present from poor taste and vulgarity than from viciousness or wrongdoing. He is, according to the description, "Powerfully built, over-dressed, jewels on his fingers, astrakhan on his collar (his errors in taste are his own affair); silent, controlled, sardonic (he can smile but he does not share the smile). An alarming man" (*LJ*, 118).

Rose's father is secretive, and some of these secrets are revealed at the end of the play: one learns about his father's death and that he has married a young girl from the brothel who is the mother of his daughter. One learns, too, of the envy he felt on visiting the Roumanian household of the young princes, to observe the talk, the laughter, and the love between the beautiful mother and Ferdinand, especially as a young boy. This envy and admiration for the lovely lady prompted him to take the painting and to want a daughter who would look and behave like his ideal. He has never communicated to Rose who his ideal is or what her qualities are; Rose is only vaguely aware that her father compares her with some standard of which she feels she falls short. One never learns why Mrs. Webster, although Portal's wife, is not allowed to behave like a wife but serves as a lady valet, dressed in servant's clothing, or why he does not discard her if he is ashamed of her, or why she is not allowed to let Rose know that she is her mother. She loves Portal, she admits, in a sudden outburst at the end and is often jealous of Rose. Indeed, her behavior is curt, cool, businesslike, with touches of dry humor, but the overall impression is disagreeable. She strikes one as an artificial, unconvincing character.

As in *Lottie Dundass* and *The Chalk Garden*, *The Last Joke* includes a past crime, a murder. In *The Last Joke*, however, the person responsible, Edward Portal, does not seem likely to pay for his misdeeds. He will give up the stolen picture, perhaps, to Hugo, but no one suggests that he be arrested or go to jail. He is to be Hugo's father-in-law, and now that the cat is out of the bag, so to speak, Mrs. Webster may become the real Mrs. Portal in all respects, and with Ferdinand

lying on the ground, happily dead, there indeed seems to be a satisfactory conclusion, but the ending is not so happy as it is bizarre. All
of act 3 seems slightly askew, and the characters of Portal and Mrs.
Webster turn into beings alien to their former selves. The sudden
revelations are artificial and jarring. In a murder mystery when the
plot concentrates on the solving of the crime, revelations, however
unusual, may be expected and in keeping with the tone and mood of
the piece.

Here, the emphasis of act 1 is on Ferdinand and his desire for death
in conjunction with the intellectual curiosity about the formula of
God. The matter of the portrait comes up near the end of the act. All
of act 2, aside from minor pursuit of the Hugo/Rose affair, deals with
Ferdinand's efforts to recover the painting, with no carryover of act
1's content. In act 3, with the picture recovered, aside from threatening to shoot at it to get a response from Portal, Ferdinand is not concerned with the painting. The emphasis again is on a continuation of
the act 1 drama; this time the thrust is on the working out of the
suicide while keeping Hugo from following after. To tie up the romance quickly, Ferdinand gives Rose a ring—that belonged to his
mother—with the notion that this will encourage Hugo to seal the
marriage bargain. This action is also jarring since Hugo and Rose
have known each other for only a week and Ferdinand has been insist-
ing on the princely pride of a family line six hundred years old. He
is now willing to ignore the family honor by allowing his brother to
marry an unstable girl with parents of less-than-humble origins and
unsavory character, rich though they may be. In other words, Ferdinand is not consistent. Acts 1 and 2 sustain suspense and dramatic
interest, but act 3 falls apart because it is not consistent in plot or
characterization with what has gone before.

There is still much to be admired in the play with its colorful characters and vivid, witty diaglogue. Enid Bagnold worked on the play
off and on over a six-year period, and when it was finished, everyone
seemed pleased with it, sure of its success. Glen Byam-Shaw, the director, had just come from a term of directorship of Shakespeare plays
at Stratford, and the sets were beautiful, Bagnold said. She had
wanted John Gielgud to play the part of Portal; he, however, was interested only in Prince Ferdinand.

The playwright felt it essential to the end of the play that the suicide be by poison, but Gielgud apparently preferred shooting himself

amid fireworks, which the director said could be done, given the ball setting; obligingly, Bagnold wrote in the revolver. There were to be many changes in the script.

A major complication arose when Sir Ralph Richardson wanted to play the part of Portal, which she felt he was unsuited for, but the box office sales, they knew, would benefit by yet another star. Richardson was in Cyprus making a film when rehearsals began, but when he returned, he had established his own ideas about the character and the blocking of scenes. There were problems with interpretation in the third act, and on tour both major actors were rewriting lines.

The critics in their denunciations of the play and especially of act 3 overlooked the good points of the first two acts, Bagnold felt. In *Autobiography* she protests the unfairness of the wholesale condemnation that drama critics use, saying nothing constructive about a play that has failed.

Noel Coward makes the following observation on *The Last Joke* in his diary (9 October 1960): "Last week John [Gielgud] and Ralph [Richardson] opened in Enid Bagnold's play and the whole thing got the most terrible notices I have ever read, much much worse than I got, and unanimous. As it is a very expensive production and at the Phoenix, which is a big theatre to fill, this looks like a disaster for Binkie [Hugh Beaumont, the producer] . . ."[2]

Among Enid Bagnold's last words on the play were her suspicions that Antoine's ghost was enjoying the spectacular ruins. Antoine had died in 1951, and she had written his obituary for the Paris paper. They had been friends for nearly forty years.

The Chinese Prime Minister

Enid Bagnold finished the first draft of *The Chinese Prime Minister* in 1961 shortly before the death of her husband. Roderick had been good at understanding the effects she was after and recognizing superfluous elements. She sent the first version of the play to her agent in New York, and later a representative of Alfred Lunt and Lynn Fontanne contacted her, suggesting she visit the Lunts' home. They would be ideal, she knew, for the leading parts.

In the meantime Roderick had become seriously ill and, not long after, died; she was shaken by the loss. Gradually, as she began her life again, she knew that she wanted to make the daily routine simpler, to shuck unneeded responsibilities. Much of what she felt now was incorporated into later versions of the play. Responsibilities, she was sure, interfered with artistic perception and inspiration.

In the play the luxury of having no demands, of existing as one pleases, is experienced especially by Bent, the old family butler; he is so old in fact (over a hundred) that he appears to be a legendary, mystic character. For five months the lady of the house has been gone and no one has needed him. He says: "Five months. (To her—with strange joy.) Five months of my own—what I never had before!—The sun and the moon passing over me . . . And nobody saying to me the dinner's ready—nor the morning's come!—And it isn't being *alone* that makes the difference!—It's being *alone—without Time!*"[3]

Enid Bagnold in the summer of 1962 was almost seventy-three, and the main character in her play is a successful actress nearing seventy. Casting the part was to be a problem. A director had come from New York, eager to work with her on the play; but he wanted to make changes, which she tried to do, though not always pleased with the suggestions. This was the beginning of a difficult period, one that playwrights experience, no doubt, despite the harmony of the initial relationship between writer and director.

She received an invitation to visit the Lunts at their country home in Wisconsin and was charmed with the imagination and grace with which they lived. Although they were in their seventies, they seemed ageless. Evidently they felt the same about her. At first her mission was to talk about *The Chinese Prime Minister* and to hope that they would come out of retirement to do the play; indeed they were interested, although Alfred Lunt preferred the part of the butler to the obvious one of the eccentric husband; in the end the joys of leisure and retirement proved greater, as they declined the roles but kept the friend.

Eventually Margaret Leighton, a much younger actress, accepted the role, and Alan Webb was cast as the butler. Bagnold, Leighton, and Webb left England for rehearsals in New York; from the beginning there were differences between Bagnold and the director in regard to meanings. They both had much at stake, and though she had resolved to be quiet, eventually she could not. For her, the play represented a depth of experience, and she would do battle for it. The director, on the other hand, also had much to lose; he had a career at stake.

Their first Boston review was bad. From this point on she became an enemy of the director by speaking out and, with Alan Webb's help, she made Leighton realize that this was a comedy. By the end of the second week the same Boston reviewer came again but now had a positive impression of the play.

Her son Tucker had come to New York for the opening, 2 January 1964; fortunately for all, the night was a success. According to Bagnold, Margaret Leighton worked her magic, and both she and the play glittered. It ran thereafter until 4 April 1964 for 108 performances.

The action takes place in the London home of a successful actress, sixty-nine going on seventy, just finishing her career. The drawing room is the setting for all three acts. The time is the present, the first scene of act 1 beginning in the evening, one hour before she is due to leave for the theater. The actress is not given a name, simply called *She* in the script, "Mama" by her children—two sons and two daughters-in-law, and "m'lady" by the elderly butler. The play may be termed a comedy of manners but with serious elements; the plot and characters are exaggerated and stylized.

As the play opens, the actress is with her married son Oliver, age twenty-nine, awaiting the arrival of the elder son Tarver who is bringing with him his surprise fiancée. Mysterious phone calls arrive throughout the two scenes of act 1. The father of the family, Sir Gregory, who has walked out on them twenty-nine years before and is supposedly dead (so the children have been told), telephones her. Bent, the butler, receives the calls, and occasionally the actress takes the phone, speaks only a phrase or two and then hangs up, pretending it is a wrong number but secretly pleased at his efforts to contact her; she receives baskets of flowers.

Tarver arrives with his girlfriend Alice, a seventeen-year-old with a distinct personality, quite different from the beautiful, sophisticated girl usually considered Tarver's type. Oliver and his wife are living with his mother. His wife Roxane, an extremely attractive young lady, comes and goes as she pleases, and, as the play progresses, shows a compulsion for love and admiration that brings her to picking up strangers on the street.

As scene 1 ends, and as it is the last night of the play, the actress suddenly decides to make this also the night of her retirement. Scene 2 of act 1 takes place approximately five months later. In the meantime, *She* is a bit disappointed with her retirement, Oliver and his wife have moved out, Alice and Tarver have married, and even Old Bent, fond of young women, has married.

Scene 2 takes place on the morning of the actress's seventieth birthday. She has ordered her own cake; Oliver arrives late because he has had to bail out Alice for shoplifting which she did simply for revenge against Tarver. Tarver, wanting nothing to do with Alice, has come by himself, and she shows up escorted by a wealthy boxer named Red Gus Risko, whom she has just met in a pub. Both sons' marriages are obviously in trouble. The actress, who often exaggerates and is seeking attention, tells her family that she has had lovers in the past and surprising her with one of them was the cause of her husband's leaving. They tend not to believe her, whereupon, in a dramatic gesture, she tells Bent to call Sir Gregory at the Savoy, where (one discovers later) he has been staying for the past five months. Otherwise he has been in Arabia for twenty-nine years as consultant to an oil-wealthy sheik. Speaking only a few words to him, she invites him to dinner that night. The scene ends with eveyone shocked to find that the father, the mystery man, is alive.

Act 2 opens that evening. Sir Gregory arrives and Bent, a bit befuddled, thinks it is Sir Gregory's father. Sir Gregory is an energetic, dynamic, wealthy gentleman. Talk of the past discloses a coolness on his part toward Oliver and an ambivalence about what happened on the evening he walked out. Tarver suddenly realizes that the oil company he works for belongs to his father. The troubles between the two young married couples flare up with verbal battles between Alice—who has again arrived with the boxer—and Tarver; Roxane's arrival creates tension when she states that Sir Gregory "picked her up" the night before, although, one is assured, nothing happened. Roxane gravitates toward the boxer, and he, with a championship fight in four days, is instantly smitten. Sir Gregory must leave for Arabia the next day, and he persuades his wife to come with him. Fighting as they always have and uncertain about what she is doing, she finally gets together a makeup case and, with an empty birdcage which she insists on taking, they leave as the curtain falls.

Act 3 takes place five months later in the afternoon. The boxer arrives, concerned about Roxane. They have had a brief affair, and he has lost his championship bout. Bent is in the house; he has come there to die, he says. Then the actress and Sir Gregory arrive. He wants to sell the house and travel. It develops that their sudden return to England was prompted by the sheik's indicating no further need of him. Alice comes in with news that she is pregnant and that she and Tarver for the present are on peaceful terms; talk of the past now reveals that, on that fateful night twenty-nine years before, the actress may have wished for an affair but in the hate of love, angry at Sir Gregory, exaggerated the event. He, believing her (that Oliver is indeed his son), asks Oliver to go back to Arabia with him after cables arrive indicating new oil fields have developed and he is needed; Oliver, however, will remain here and cope with the returned, still vulnerable Roxane. The actress has already determined that she wishes to remain in her house by herself and indulge in the pleasure of no responsibilities. As the play ends, she and Bent are left alone and apparently happy to be so.

The characters in this play have strong egos; they are trying to deal with needs but their wills clash. Alice and Tarver are much like Strindberg characters. There is an excess of anger and violence in their relationship, the same type of hate-love seen in several of Strindberg's people. Their emotions are so intense that these two may injure each other physically or torture each other mentally in a fight to the death. Similar behavior seems to have been part of the relationship between the actress and her husband to a lesser degree in the past, but the older couple possessed sensibilities, self-confidence, and a sense of humor that the young couple lack. Alice does not hide her feelings; and in anger and revenge she purposely shoplifts a handbag so that her arrest will embarrass Tarver and damage his career. Her youth may be part of her frustration and inability to cope, but Tarver, much older than she, does nothing to help resolve the conflicts or provide understanding.

All of the characters suffer from a lack of communication. The two who most nearly understand each other are Oliver and his mother. They share a closeness that the others do not have. Oliver, his mother's favorite, is kind, loving, and thoughtful; he adores his wife Roxane but does not know how to please her or satisfy her need for admiration. She desires the attention of many men and yet comes to realize that this compulsion is destructive. Her character is much like that of Serena Blandish who enjoys saying yes to men. Roxane might be a sequel to Serena, for Roxane has the money and the husband that Serena longs for and sees as the answer to her dreams, but money and a loving mate apparently are not enough.

The main character, *She,* has a full life and much attention, which she still requires, and, she is annoyed when the others are occupied with their own problems; they seem willing to believe that her life is downhill hereafter. In answer to Oliver's question about a group of

playscripts, she says, "I haven't read them. I haven't *opened* them!
Those lines—those words! . . . Oh—why does no one write *real*
plays—about the fascination and disaster of being old!" Oliver wants
to know what the fascination is. "What might lie ahead of me! If I
had the daring . . ." she says. He asks then about the disaster of being old. She replies, "What you all expect for me! That for me it's
the end of surprises! For me it's the final run-in" (*CPM,* 173–74).

Nevertheless, she discovers in the five-month period after her retirement that she has lost an important aspect of her life. An act of
folly, she considers it, and she tells Bent that she has gained nothing
by it. Being seventy was a mountain she wanted to explore, but she
has been in public so long that she doesn't know how to lead this
private life. "Without the theatre I feel diminished. Caught in so
small a programme! I put on clothes. I take them off. Eat. Sleep.
And in between . . . No sense of God!" (*CPM,* 185). The reference
to God is a bit ambiguous. She says she expected some sign from
God, but why or for what one never discovers. She is not religious in
the usual sense, leaning rather toward an Eastern philosophy and way
of thinking such as wishing to meet a Chinese Prime Minister.

Once she has come back from Arabia, she has resigned herself apparently to further withdrawal from public life and from the little red
engagement book, ready to live by herself and revel in the loss of responsibility and routine. At the moment she longs for this type of
life, but can *She,* as she complained earlier, really be content out of
the public eye? Enid Bagnold would have us believe so, for the play
ends on a positive note with the young couples in a temporary armistice and *She* ready to explore the sensations of living and the pleasures of the senses. She spoke earlier of the fascination ahead, if she
has the daring. Perhaps the daring involves withdrawal to the sym-
bolic mountain and time for looking at life. The fact that the actress
has no name other than *She* suggests that she is a universal figure and
could be any seventy-year-old woman discovering herself alone but excited over the prospect of adventures to come, not wanting to lose her
life in routine, anticipating perhaps a rebirth of the spirit. In the
British version of the play with the changes in rewriting, the actress
is given the name Mrs. Forrest. Except for satisfying Dame Edith Evans, who was playing the part, the name seems to add little if anything to the character.

Of all of Bagnold's butlers, Bent is the oldest, the oddest, and the
funniest. He is a mystic character with an old body and a young spirit

but quite stubborn and determined. He has made friends with death. Twice during the play he seems to have expired but revives again; once the characters put a screen around him and for a time forget he is there, presuming him dead. Later he comes back to life. Despite his age, he has a vigorous interest in women and sex, but, because of his age, he becomes something of a wise man making significant pronouncements. His words of wisdom to the actress as she comes back from Arabia are: "Don't do things twice," meaning in this case, don't try marriage again with Sir Gregory. The fact that Bent carries on the same duties that he has performed for fifty years or that he is working at all at his age is preposterous, but then the presentation is not realistic.

Bent is one of the chief sources of humor in the play. One or two critics have indicated rightly that Bent is reminiscent of Firs (Fiers, Feers) in Chekhov's *The Cherry Orchard*. Old Firs (eighty-seven), also too old to be an active servant, is humorous in his deafness and mistaken responses to the other characters and in his solicitous behavior toward them, but he is more realistic than Bent and more pathetic. At the end of the Chekhov play, when the others have left the house and locked the doors, not realizing that he is still there, Firs lies down to rest and presumably to die. The mistress will not be coming back. His concerns are for the others, but he also mumbles, "Life has gone by, as if I hadn't lived at all." In this play Bent lies down, alone in the house when the actress leaves with Sir Gregory for Arabia. The furniture is covered with dust sheets. For five months he is alone, but for him this has been a gift of timelessness, a luxury of no demands; he is discovered under the dust sheets at the beginning of act 3; a major difference between him and Firs is that Bent gets up and prepares happily to live on and again serve the returned lady of the house.

Sir Gregory is a vivid, strong old man, decisive, outspoken, with some marvelous, witty lines. He is a man of action but, when need be, is chivalrous and tender to his wife. What he wants most, she forces him to admit at the end, is to get back into the business world of the sheik. He is eager then to leave for Arabia and to resume his former active life.

He and she have battled throughout their married life as they did in the recent five months together, and yet they love each other. By the end of the play he has accepted the fact that he was wrong in walking out twenty-nine years before, but he also loves the life he led during those years. Sir Gregory has the energy and the breezy humor of a Bernard Shaw character. He reminds one of Andrew Undershaft, the munitions tycoon of *Major Barbara,* a vigorous, larger-than-life man who also walked out on his family to become immensely wealthy and then reappear many years later.

The humor in the play stems mainly from the clever dialogue and from the characterizations of Bent, the actress, Sir Gregory, and to a lesser extent, Alice and the boxer, Red Gus Risko. For example, in act 1, scene 1, a mysterious phone call arrives and the actress after pooh-poohing Bent's announcement that it is the deceased Sir Gregory, takes the phone but is anxious to get out of Oliver's hearing range and to keep Bent from saying any more. She says, "I know what it is—it's about a hat . . ." Bent says, "No, it isn't." She asks into the phone, "Who's speaking? . . . Ten—what? Ten—orchids. Ten—DOZEN! (Putting her hand over the telephone she holds it away from her for a moment. Then, suddenly) I wish they were for me—but I'm afraid they're not!" (Replaces instrument on stand.) Oliver asks, "Is it love?" She answers, "Of course it's love—but he had the wrong number" (*CPM,* 172).

A few lines later, Oliver says to Bent, "Take it from me! My father's been dead twenty years." Bent says, "I know it. But that doesn't stop him ringing" (*CPM,* 172–3).

When Oliver has bailed out Alice after the shoplifting incident, the actress asks, "What shop was it?" Bent answers, "Fortnums." Then she says to Oliver, "Ring Cazan. The solicitor. He gets everyone out of scrapes. No—wait. He was buried yesterday . . . That's why I thought of him! . . . (*CPM,* 188).

Later, with all present awaiting Sir Gregory, the doorbell rings. Bent goes to the door but returns, scared, holding the door shut against someone behind him. He says, "It's Sir Gregory's . . . father, m'lady . . . It's your ladyship's . . . father-in-law . . . " (*CPM,* 204). Sir Gregory almost pushes Bent down as he bursts open the door, contending that he would need to be a hundred and twenty to be her father-in-law!

He has brought her a small case of diamonds which he opens, and, as Alice comes close to see, he asks, "Who are *you?*" Alice replies (on guard), "Don't you know?" He says, "Yes, I do!—Shocking!—Your face was in the newspapers. (To his wife) How beautifully you touch jewels! (Glances at Alice) But keep them away from the Shop-Lifter!" (*CPM,* 205).

Just after Sir Gregory arrives, the actress tells Bent to go and sit in her bedroom. Then as it is time to carve the turkey, she calls for him. He has found her bottle of gin behind the mirror and comes out, hair standing on end, drunk. He says he has had a dream about his first love—on a pond, skating, and in talking about the incident he "skates" around the room.

Although humor is present throughout the play, it occurs in patches, alternating with serious elements.

A few significant symbols are important to the play's theme and plot. One has to do with the concept of the Chinese Prime Minister, another with the empty birdcage, and still another with a particular chair in the drawing room.

There are several facets of the Chinese Prime Minister image as the actress uses the term. Sometimes she is speaking of another person who is wise, free-spirited, poetic, and loving. At the end *She* is the person, having acquired the wisdom and daring to be a free spirit. The actress in her last role is playing a wise woman; in her own life she feels she knows nothing. "What do I know of a private life! I've been defrauded," she says to Oliver "I wish I could meet a Chinese Prime Minister . . . In the East—when age was near Paradise and not a prison." This would not be one in office but one who makes a triumph of his retirement. "He writes poems that will outlive his achievements! He carries a bird cage. We go up in the mountains together" (*CPM*, 182).

Later in act 1 when she feels that her sons have outgrown her, she says, "I should like to be a miracle—as I used to be!" and to Oliver she says with a quiver, "You must find me the Chinese Prime Minister" (*CPM*, 194).

Near the end of act 2 when Sir Gregory says that he will take her away to Arabia, she comments quietly to Oliver that it might be the prime minister. Of Sir Gregory she asks, "Do we go up into the mountains together?" (*CPM*, 223). He doesn't understand her meaning. The last reference comes near the end of the play after Sir Gregory leaves. She waves to him and says to herself, "He is looking forward again! But I am going to make Time stand still! . . . It is *I* who am the Chinese Prime Minister" (*CPM*, 245). She feels triumphant in her decision and in her knowledge; it seems that she does not need anyone else to provide her with love, guidance, or wisdom. She is strong enough and confident enough now to live a creative retirement; Sir Gregory is getting off the mountain and going back into the world.

The birdcage is part of the Chinese Prime Minister's possessions. It is referred to several times. In the simple description of the set at the beginning, one is told that there is to be an empty birdcage somewhere in the room. Also, when she leaves with Sir Gregory, the two objects she insists on taking are the makeup case and the birdcage. One might make any number of guesses as to the meaning of the birdcage; perhaps the cage symbolizes her structured life from which her spirit is freed. Or is Sir Gregory the bird who has flown from the cage of marriage?

The chair, another symbol, is the subject of much speculation. Supposedly the actress and her lover were sitting in that chair on the fateful night of the big quarrel; the actress in a sudden burst of revelation to her family, talking about her lovers, says: "They all had the same reactions to me. Instantaneous, unmistakable!—And then—that *other—unrefusable* man! It was with him your father caught me! (She begins to laugh.) It was in this chair—with the mended leg. Your father broke it! Bent was just bringing in the coffee. . ." (*CPM,* 198). Oliver is upset by her story, but Alice points out that she has gained what she wanted—their attention.

Later on in act 2 when Sir Gregory moves backward to avoid the drunken Bent, he upsets the chair. Bent turns, pointing to it, saying, "You know what happened. . . " (*CPM,* 211). This time Sir Gregory bursts into laughter. Bent speaks vaguely about love and quarrels and fisticuffs. Oliver asks what happened to the man, and Sir Gregory says, "I hit him." Bent declares that Sir Gregory tried to get the name from him, but Bent ate the calling card. Bent says of the actress that "she was in a hurricane of temper. . . " (*CPM,* 212). The subject is changed as Bent prepares to carve the turkey. Finally in act 3 the subject comes up again after *She* has told Sir Gregory that they are like two old lions and that they waste each other in the battle to be right. He asks then about the singer's name. He can't remember and in fact she can't either. He says then, "It was in *that chair* you told me!" and she answers, "In the momentary hate of love I might have said anything!" He persists, "Was he your lover?" and she replies, "I had the wish. (Musing.) But did it happen?" (*CPM,* 239). At this response Sir Gregory roars with laughter, satisfied that she had been fantasizing. He no longer doubts that he is Oliver's father.

The theme of freedom of the spirit and exploring the sensations of living is prevalent throughout the play, emerging again and again in the actress's speeches, but, until the end, there is uncertainty about what she really wants and thinks she can achieve. As Sir Gregory leaves, however, she tells Bent she intends to "reverse the habits of a lifetime," to speculate on "Why the grey parrot talks—and not the green! How a dog can establish with me the mystery of humour!—I want to think of these things and find the springs in common there may be" (CPM, 249).

The play is ambiguous because often the lines are elliptical rather than direct, and no particular effort is made to be clear; also because Enid Bagnold speaks like a poet.

The New York production was a hit, but there was not as much success with the London production. Dame Edith Evans insisted on supplying emotion and tender feelings where they did not belong, according to Bagnold. Apparently Dame Edith did not understand the play. Opening night was on 20 May 1965. Bagnold attended with playwright Terence Rattigan and drama critic T. C. Worsley. Both understood the dilemma, and Worsley acknowledged in his review that the player's style and the play's style were at odds. It played on, but Bagnold was disappointed. After *The Chalk Garden, The Chinese Prime Minister* is the best of her plays.

Of the New York critics Walter Kerr said in the *New York Herald Tribune;* "It shimmers on the stage—like a vast insubstantial spider's web, strung with bits of real rain. The lines are thoughts, not echoes, not borrowings. And they are often so very funny. There is not a single careless line."[4]

Call Me Jacky (1968) (A Matter of Gravity—1976)

Shortly thereafter Bagnold continued work on another play with which she struggled from 1965 through 1967, a comedy with bittersweet elements. This was *Call Me Jacky*. Again, the leading lady is a contemporary, this time a grandmother with a pedigree, also with spunk and vivacity. Mrs. Basil has been leading a life of creative retirement, being in that way an extension of the actress in *The Chinese Prime Minister*. Despite her wealth, she has stripped her responsibilities and chores to the minimum and lives quietly, relishing ordinary daily experiences, keeping only one household servant, a cook.

The play takes place in her large two-hundred-year-old country home of thirty rooms, but the single set features only two rooms, the drawing room and half of the kitchen. Mrs. Basil lives in the front of the house and has been casual about its upkeep. As the play opens, a real estate agent has come to persuade her to sell some of her property. The house and garden alone would be worth about forty thousand pounds; he would pull down the house, he says, and build smaller houses on the site; she is not interested.

She receives as weekend guests her grandson Niggie, now studying at Oxford, and four of his friends. Niggie has grown up in this house under the care of his grandmother. One never learns what happened to his parents. The guests—two couples—are eccentric: Herbert, an older gentlemanly person with his young lover Tom, and Shatov, a militant, politically aggressive lady, with her attractive young friend Elizabeth from Jamaica. Niggie fears his grandmother is lonely and has invited them in order to expose her to modern ideas and attitudes. He has never met Elizabeth before and now finds himself falling in love with her.

Mrs. Basil is a gracious but commanding figure, as unusual in her own way as the other characters. Her recently hired cook, a lesbian who drinks, has just been released from an asylum and adds to the eccentricity of the household. The guests are impressed with Mrs. Basil, although she is everything that Shatov has been preaching against. She accepts them with polite, amused tolerance, pleased with her own liberality.

The guests, however, with the exception of Herbert, are rude to each other and to Mrs. Basil. Their private matters are made public. As they consider themselves intellectuals, the play becomes in part a satire on intellectuals (Shatov in particular) who espouse causes. Tom, Herbert's young lover, has been a drug addict and causes Herbert much anguish with his suicide attempts. At one point the cook, Du-Bois, kitchen knife in hand, announces that Tom has cut his throat; suspense mounts since everyone (including the audience) believes that she may have murdered him. But Tom reappears twenty minutes later with the explanation that he had hit DuBois for making a pass at him, and she had given him a superficial jab with the kitchen knife. DuBois recognizes Shatov from their school days, and it appears that Shatov, champion of the downtrodden and proud of her own supposed poverty, has grown up in riches and still is wealthy, though she spends little.

Niggie pursues his interest in Elizabeth despite Shatov's presence, but when he talks to her of love, she lets him know that her only interest is in the house. She grew up reading about England and loving the old ways and traditions. She has an obsession now with the house and makes clear that if she marries Niggie, they are to have it to live in. Mrs. Basil can live in the gatehouse which she has previously suggested for them. Mrs. Basil thinks not. After she is dead, they can have the whole estate. Niggie doesn't want the house and land, but he will do whatever Elizabeth wants.

It is discovered that Elizabeth's father in Jamaica is black. This fact does not dissuade Niggie nor cause Mrs. Basil to forbid their marriage. As act 2 ends, Elizabeth and Niggie are off to Jamaica to live. The other guests leave and DuBois is taken back to the asylum. Mysterious murders have been part of her background.

Act 3 takes place eight years later. The house has suffered further deterioration; DuBois is back again as cook. Herbert has been invited for the weekend as it is the occasion for Niggie and Elizabeth's first visit back to England. Herbert's new friend is the flamboyant real estate agent Charlie of the first act, Tom having commited suicide under someone else's patronage.

The marriage of Elizabeth and Niggie has not done well, but Niggie is determined to stick with Elizabeth. They now have two sons, one black and one white. Elizabeth is more adamant than ever about owning the house. Shatov makes a brief appearance, this time speaking of her youth, and expressing the opinion that five hundred families could be settled here. Charlie as the real estate agent again unsuccessfully seeks to buy the house and garden to make way for new houses, this time offering eighty thousand pounds.

As the play ends, Mrs. Basil, wanting to save Niggie's marriage, offers them the house and will live in the wing of the asylum designated for the sane elderly. She has been a board member of this institution for years. Before leaving, DuBois offers a chance at suicide via poisoned wine; DuBois's conviction years before, one discovers, came from helping the elderly in a nursing home to end their lives. Mrs. Basil, however, declines the invitation and, taking the cook with her, leaves.

The ending of the play seems arbitrary and artificial. The sudden abdication in favor of the unsympathetic Elizabeth rankles, especially since the decision is made on impulse, and Elizabeth has not shown herself worthy of the inheritance or even committed to making a success of her marriage.

Mrs. Basil knows that they could not live there together. She says to Elizabeth: "There is more anger than there used to be among the generations. The house is threatened. I don't know its future; but such as it is I give it to you. Bring them up here—if you can, Elizabeth! *Make* something of the black boy."[5] The little black boy apparently is especially bright and talented. Mrs. Basil shows more interest in him than in his brother although neither is present in the play. Niggie says he worships him.

Just before leaving Mrs. Basil admits to Niggie that she's as "scared of death as anyone! And when it comes . . . But it won't! Because I'm immortal. . . " (*MG,* 335). Her reference to death and her fears have not been dwelt on earlier in the play. She shows courage and determination in quickly breaking the ties to her home. She says, "There are things to which I am tied that need loosening. A trumpery and tender collection. Pieces of jade—light through the corridors, odd angles, small windows . . . I can do without them . . . I can re-invoke them!" She tells DuBois to pack her books, but she is taking nothing else. When DuBois asks about her clothes, she says, "I shall wear a nightgown." All of these are spur-of-the-moment decisions. Elizabeth wants to know if there is money to "set things right." She answers, "Yes, there is the money. But not the strength. You need youth to put order back—for a second time" (*MG,* 333).

Niggie, although seeming to understand his grandmother, remains passive, not trying to dissuade her, allowing Elizabeth to have what she wants. The last few lines are flippant as DuBois tells Mrs. Basil "I adore you," then asks, "When we get there . . . won't you call me Jacky . . ." and Mrs. Basil says, "I'll be buggered if I do" (*MG,* 336).

There are certain similarities in plot between this play and *The Cherry Orchard.* In both plays the old estates are decaying, and the new order of people unconnected with the traditions of a former way of life seek to tear down what remains of the old and build new houses in the name of progress. In *Call Me Jacky* Charlie—with his hair dyed like a daffodil—wants to tear down the house and divide the land into small plots. Shatov, too, proposes this move.

In *The Cherry Orchard* Lopakhin, the brash young businessman, a former peasant, wants to tear down the famous cherry orchard and build villas for the summer people. All of this activity is weighed in terms of money and progress. The big difference is that Mrs. Basil is still rich and need not sell whereas Chekhov's characters, Madame Ranevsky and her brother, are not, and are forced to stand by helplessly while the estate is auctioned and then bought by the enterprising Lopakhin. In both cases it is the end of an era, a cultured tradition of country houses, entertaining, and living on a grand scale. The end of Mrs. Basil's era came years before, but she has been sitting out the changes because she can afford to do so; her leaving now is for family reasons. In the Chekhov play the end of an era came with the end of serfdom, the breaking up of the estates, and the inability of the gentry to afford living in their former manner. The elderly servant Firs remembers and laments the loss of the former way of life.

At the close of *Call Me Jacky* Mrs. Basil leaves as a sacrifice to the happiness of her grandson's marriage. On the surface it would seem that the one person who appreciates the estate and its former beauty will now own it. One has no reason to believe, however, that Elizabeth, discontent with everything in the past, will ever find happiness in the rebuilding of the estate. At the end of the Chekhov play the family leave the property because they have lost it.

Since Mrs. Basil is proud of her heritage and has the money to take care of the property though not as she claims the strength, one must blame her for "letting it decay." At the beginning of act 3 the stage description indicates that "There must be a leak in the ceiling for in one corner of the room there is a two-handled zinc bath tub" (*MG*, 312). Later on, when it rains and water is running into the bathtub, "a crash of plaster is heard next door, and the rush of water." DuBois emerges from the kitchen saying, "Half the kitchen is down" and Mrs. Basil replies, "Cook in the other half" (*MG*, 330).

The characters especially Elizabeth, Shatov, Tom, and DuBois are disagreeable. Elizabeth emerges as a kind of Emma Bovary who has read romantic novels and expects to find the same picturesque life that she has longed for in her dreams. She says to the others: "Well I love this house, I love what is here. And I wish to God it was mine!" (*MG*, 300). She wonders then whether she should have said that. The question is immaterial since she goes on in an insensitive manner later to say much more, but explains now that she has avoided school but loved reading. She has read about the life of the affluent in England and loved what she read. "I admire—I adore the English," she says. "I suffer that they cut no ice! . . . . I'm a Colonial." (*MG*, 300).

It is just after this speech that DuBois, being familiar with her particular skintone, exposes her with the declaration that she is "coloured." Eight years later Elizabeth, "colder, dryer, exuberance . . . gone," according to the stage directions (*MG,* 314), admits that the marriage has not been fulfilling, and in regard to the children, she says, "I am consumed about my own life. I have hardly time for theirs. . . " (*MG,* 315). Shatov, too, retains that strong ego as she states, "I never take my eyes off—*me*—for one single minute" (*MG,* 328). Elizabeth's obsession for the house has intensified during the years; she seems driven by anger and frustration.

A familiar pattern here is the person enslaved by love with the constant threat of suicide. As in *The Last Joke* with Hugo and Ferdinand, Tom keeps Herbert in a state of anxiety. As Herbert points out, Tom's attempts are "almost-suicides" and never meant to be anything more. They are merely a means of manipulating others but they are successful nevertheless.

The satire includes the ridiculous behavior of the homosexual lovers and the artificiality of the Tom and Charlie characters. The character most strongly satirized is Shatov, the "Left and Liberal," who on the surface appears committed and strong. Yet she stutters and cannot look Mrs. Basil in the eye. Her oratory is effective only for crowds. Her hypocrisy extends to the denial of her own wealth. She insists that Mrs. Basil give up her empty acres for popular use and yet she will not disperse her father's fortune because it is his monument, and she idolized her father. Making a fortune, too, is an art, she says. She sees no similarity with Mrs. Basil's heritage, which has been intact for two hundred years. Her significant ideas become empty and meaningless, and as Elizabeth points out, "She sucks up" to the modern times, to the age, doing and becoming what is fashionable—"Left and Liberal." Thus, the satire extends to all pseudointellectuals.

The DuBois character is a source of humor often, but she is also sinister, creating suspense with her kitchen knife, her mysterious past, and obviously maniacal nature. In her shady aspects she is like a Harold Pinter character. She longs to communicate on friendly terms with Mrs. Basil whom she adores. "Call me Jacky," she says, sometimes as a threat. Part of Mrs. Basil's reluctance to do so is not mere snobbishness but a necessity to keep the upper hand and to direct her behavior into acceptable channels.

Mrs. Basil seems to see a need for offering work situations to unfortunate people. There is a certain rootlessness and aloneness about her,

for she no longer seems to have connections with other family or social ties with members of her own class. The builder and the plumber
come in on the evenings when it rains and they sit drinking and talking, Mrs. Basil tells Niggie.

Niggie is the straightest character in the play, a foil for the talk
and behavior of the others. He loves his grandmother and is not impressed with wealth or possessions but once he has committed himself
to Elizabeth, he remains loyal to her. It is difficult to tell if he is a
weak character, whether his need to hang onto Elizabeth is due to his
own immaturity and lack of direction or whether he loves Elizabeth
and wants to be a part of her life despite her complaints. He says, "I
say nothing. I listen to her. I have heard it all before. There is no
end of an end to her discontent. She sees the worst in everything and
that is the worst you can have." He says he is too tired to change
(partners), but he admits also, "She is all I have in the world. She is
my one throw of marriage and I have lost on it. But I *know* her. What
is terrible is to know no one" (*MG,* 320).

The humor in the play comes from the characterizations, the dialogue, and sometimes the stage business. As in *The Chalk Garden* and
to a lesser extent *The Chinese Prime Minister,* in *Call Me Jacky* Bagnold
makes generous use of aphorisms in Oscar Wilde fashion. Mrs. Basil
says, "The only thing we never expect is the truth" (*MG,* 307). She
says to Elizabeth, "A murderess is only an ordinary woman in a temper" (*MG,* 330–331). When Charlie, the real estate agent, tells her
she could also have a flat in London, she says, "I don't really care
about London. It is so up to date about nothing" (*MG,* 260).

When Niggie first tells her about Shatov, the political woman, he
mentions that Shatov would consider flowers in her bedroom as frivolous nor would she want to take a tour of the house which Mrs. Basil
considers beautiful. Niggie borrows Shatov's attitudes when he says,
"One has no right to beauty," but his grandmother protests, asking
if he is quoting; if not, she says "it's the silliest thing I've ever heard
you say!" (*MG,* 267). Niggie again reflects their thinking when he
says, "I'm upset by the state of the world," to which Mrs. Basil replies, "The state of the world depends on one's newspaper" (*MG,*
267). These flip comments are not meant to be taken seriously of
course but gems of wisdom appear also. Mrs. Basil, talking about the
house, tells Shatov, "I noticed long ago with so-called inanimate objects that they are not inanimate at all. They're bluffing! They cry for
attention! You must ignore them—cars—for instance!" (*MG,* 271).

When Mrs. Basil tells Niggie that she inherited the house from her grandmother and that she believes in family and tradition and the past, Niggie tells her, "Darling—be modern," and she replies, "I've been modern. I got tired of it" (*MG,* 279).

The other characters make use of aphorisms also. Elizabeth, earlier in the play, showing her impatience with sex, said, "I don't need it. Sex is just an old carrot used by God to get children. . ." (*MG,* 290).

Elizabeth's values contrast with those of Mrs. Basil, despite her love of the house and all things English. She asks Mrs. Basil in act 2, "Do you know what girls want?" Mrs. Basil says, "In my day love," to which Elizabeth replies, "In my day security. I've never been in love. Jewels, cosmetics . . . to spend, to attract . . . social position" (*MG,* 300). Elizabeth is brutally honest and one sees little of her charm. Worse, her character never improves. She is even more disagreeable eight years later and seemingly more bitter, willing Mrs. Basil to get on with it: drop dead or move out.

At its presentation in 1968 the play received no hurrahs, but it was not ignored. It was published in 1970 with three other Bagnold plays in a separate volume and eight years later with several changes and a different title. Now called *A Matter of Gravity,* it became a starring vehicle for Katharine Hepburn and opened in New York at the Broadhurst Theater on 3 February 1976.

At Irene Selznick's suggestion, Miss Hepburn had contacted Enid Bagnold while on a trip to London, and thereafter over the years a friendly relationship continued. Irene felt that they would be kindred spirits and evidently she was right. She had originally wanted Katharine Hepburn to play Madrigal in *The Chalk Garden,* but Miss Hepburn had declined the part.

In *A Matter of Gravity* among the changes from the original play the biggest were in the role of the cook DuBois. She no longer is a threat to the lives of the other characters nor has there been murder in her past. Besides being an alcoholic, her major oddity now is that she has the power to levitate herself; sometimes, even when she doesn't care to. At one point she ties the doorstop around her waist to hold herself down, but loses it and up she goes. This happens off-stage, of course. However, it is this "miracle" that allows Mrs. Basil to believe that this mystery may be a ladder to other mysteries, and ultimately something she can believe in. She wants to believe in God and now considers the possibility that there are superior forces, and if she doesn't completely believe, she hopes that God will be fair enough to forgive her.

In the first act the real estate agent offers her the handsome sum of

£240,000 for her property as opposed to the £80,000 offered in the earlier play eight years before, demonstrating the powers of inflation no doubt. Neither does the real estate agent come back as Herbert's new friend Charlie. One never meets his new friend.

In the later version there is less emphasis on the deterioration of the house. In fact, Mrs. Basil and Jacky are working on the improvement of the kitchen as the play begins. When the guests arrive, there is less general talk. Shatov at the end seems to give over her political philosophy when she admits to buying a new house with a pool and also horses.

The name Niggie has been changed to Nickie, a part played on Broadway by Christopher Reeve of Superman fame. When Nickie proposes to Elizabeth, it is she who offers the information that her father is black. Elizabeth is still as disagreeable as she was in the earlier play but at the end when Mrs. Basil says that she will leave the house to her grandson, Elizabeth indicates that though there has been no love involved, she will try to make Nickie happy and will devote herself to the house.

Their arrival in England is the result of a letter sent to Nickie by Herbert, indicating that Mrs. Basil needs psychiatric attention, since she seems to think her cook can fly.

At the beginning of the printed version of the play, Enid Bagnold included a note of interest regarding the role of Mrs. Basil as played by Katharine Hepburn. She says: "Though through an accident Miss Katharine Hepburn—who created the leading role in "A Matter of Gravity"—was forced to use a wheelchair, yet, curiously enough, this added another dimension to the characterization. Naturally it is left to the discretion of any future director or actress as to whether this change should be repeated."[6]

From newspaper reviews came these intriguing captions: "That Hepburn Magic Wins Broadway Again" (Christian Science Monitor); "Kate in Loonie Land" (New York Daily News); "Comedy of Bad Manners" (Newsweek); " "A Matter of Gravity' Enshrines Hepburn" (New York Times). In general, the critics fell under the Hepburn spell but did not appreciate the play.

Of the positive reviews, Martin Gottfried in the New York Post (4 February 1976) wrote:

It is not often these days that a play is written with grace in pursuit of intelligence. Both seem out of fashion. "A Matter of Gravity" (not a new play but new to America) is hardly in the class of her wonderful "The Chalk Gar-

den," or the lesser "The Chinese Prime Minister," but time spent with even
an untidy Enid Bagnold play is time spent in the company of intellectual
finesse. That seems to me time well spent by any measure. Especially with
Katharine Hepburn in the bargain. . . ."

He admits that the play's sociological points are in confusion but he
goes on to say:

Ah, but the dialogue, Bagnold writes with such wit, and such sense, that
she makes wisdom and civility seem like long lost treasures that must be
returned to our lives at once, lest we die of stupidity. Even when nothing is
happening, which is most of the time, the flow of observation and humor is
invigorating. And though it is actionless there is a theater of language to the
play . . . Nor is the charm and wisdom of this play to be dismissed out of
hand. Between its championship of intelligence and the radiance of Hepburn, "A Matter of Gravity" is not mere matinee theater. It may not be first
rate but it is certainly first class.[7]

Among the plays appearing on Broadway at the same time were
Peter Shaffer's *Equus,* Alan Ayckbourn's *The Norman Conquests,* and
Tom Stoppard's *Travesties. A Matter of Gravity* played for a limited
engagement of seventy-nine performances and closed on 10 April
1976; however, a road company, also starring Katharine Hepburn,
began its tour in Denver on 29 September and finished eight months
later in Baltimore.

Chapter Nine
Afterwords and Conclusions

In each succeeding novel Enid Bagnold's main characters grew with her. Their age was her age and often their story was largely her own or that of the people she knew well. The young nurse's aide of *A Diary without Dates* became the more mature volunteer with the Englishwomen drivers for the French Army in *The Happy Foreigner*. The Serena Blandish prototype was the sister of a friend of hers, but the Flor di Folio environment and the personalities of that set were of Bagnold's own experience. She was now the more sophisticated lady entering a sparkling, fun-loving international society. Later as the mother with children and the horse show family, she became in one sense the mother in *National Velvet* but also the child from her own Jamaica days, her daughter Laurian emerging as the main model for Velvet. Again, she was the mother with family, about to have another child, a still more mature woman with household problems and responsibilities in a wealthy family, identifying with the main character of *The Squire*. In her autumn years and with aging friends she chose as her subjects in *The Loved and Envied* people in their sixties and seventies, with a leading character patterned after her dear friend, Diana Manners Cooper.

An overlap occurred with her first two plays, which were produced before *The Loved and Envied,* but once this novel was finished, her interest in novel writing ended. From then on she became the playwright, and even though *Lottie Dundass, Poor Judas,* and *The Last Joke* were suggested by experiences, the more successful plays were those in which the leading characters were extensions of her own age and personality: Mrs. St. Maugham of *The Chalk Garden,* the actress of *The Chinese Prime Minister,* and Mrs. Basil of *Call Me Jacky/A Matter of Gravity.* The leading roles are difficult because they carry so much responsibility for the plays; but they are also an aging actress's dream.

Characterization

Certain character types appear repeatedly in her work. One is the strong mother or grandmother figure, beginning with Araminty

Brown of *National Velvet* and including the squire, Lady Ruby Maclean of *The Loved and Envied*, Mrs. Dundass, Mrs. St. Maugham, the actress of *The Chinese Prime Minister*, and Mrs. Basil. At the same time, often the father figure is missing. In the two plays that do feature male figures, Edward Walker of *Poor Judas* and Edward Portal of *The Last Joke*, the father is a negative force, unsympathetic and flawed in character. Walker betrays his collaborator on their book and lives a lie, pretending to be what he is not; and Edward Portal, having murdered his father years before, is seen as ruthless and, one suspects, dishonest in the acquisition of his art treasures. Neither Walker nor Portal has a mate in the normal sense. Walker's wife has died years before, and Portal's wife is not treated as an equal, but is relegated to the role of servant.

With the absence of partners or close family ties, most of Enid Bagnold's main characters tend to be loners, often isolated from others in their environment. That is true also of the younger women in *A Diary without Dates*, *The Happy Foreigner*, and *Serena Blandish*, in addition to Miranda in *The Loved and Envied*, and Jenny in *Poor Judas*, Rose in *The Last Joke*, and, of course, Madrigal in *The Chalk Garden*.

The happiest works are those in which the characters communicate and are content with their lot, as in the two novels of the middle years, *National Velvet* and *The Squire*. Here the family ties and spirit remain strong.

In addition to the strong female figure, the other character type appearing most often in the novels and plays is the eccentric but influential butler. The butlers begin with Martin in *Serena Blandish*. He becomes Serena's confidant, gives her advice and provides bits of cynical wisdom that show his experience in the way of the world. Hard as he tries, he cannot fathom Serena's inability to act on his advice. He has, at the same time, a sense of humor that takes into account the weaknesses of human nature. The butler in *The Squire*, a dour individual, is (as are most of the butlers) a remnant of a society that is changing rapidly and no longer requires the ritual of the past. He admits to the squire that many of his colleagues become alcoholics, as is his replacement while he is on holiday.

Most of the butlers are sources of comedy. Pinkbell of *The Chalk Garden* is the exception; his ominous presence is felt but he never appears on stage. Old Matthew in *The Last Joke* shows the loyalty to his masters Hugo and Ferdinand that all butlers of former ages were supposed to feel for their employers for whom they had worked a lifetime. In the same play Mrs. Webster functions as a valet for Edward

Portal, providing for that reason a bizarre touch. Bent, the aged butler in *The Chinese Prime Minister,* is a fantasy figure, the butler at the
end of his days, allowed to show his whimsical nature but still in service and still needed. In *Call Me Jacky* as in *The Last Joke* the servant
figure becomes a woman, in this case, a butler-and-cook combination,
even more eccentric than those in previous works. She drinks, is
sloppy, is potentially menacing, and in *A Matter of Gravity* levitates.

For the purpose of suspense, several of the works contain a mysterious person with a questionable past. Count Montague D'Costa of *Serena Blandish* is a good example. No one knows anything about him
except that he is wealthy. His real background is an important element in maintaining the suspense of the novel, which becomes most
intense at the end so that when the truth of his parentage is revealed,
everyone is shocked (present-day society would not have found the situation as shocking). Mi Taylor in *National Velvet* keeps his previous
background a secret. One never knows why or what happened to cut
short his involvement with the racing world. Madrigal in *The Chalk
Garden* remains a mystery, for even at the end of the play one does
not know whether she has committed murder. Edward Portal's past
includes secrecy and murder as does that of Du Bois in *Call Me Jacky.*

Regarding Plot and Theme

Not every novel or play need have a specific theme, Enid Bagnold
felt. The plays, especially, tend to present experience for the sake of
experience. It is difficult to identify clear-cut themes for *Lottie Dundass, The Last Joke, The Chinese Prime Minister,* or *Call Me Jacky/A
Matter of Gravity.*

There are, aside from form, some significant differences between
the novels and the plays. The plays tend to be more whimsical and
fanciful with weaker plots. Plotting was not one of Bagnold's strong
points. She was more concerned with the language of a play than with
the story line. In this respect, Irene Selznick speaks of their first encounter while working together on *The Chalk Garden:* "At our first
session I had disconcerted her by asking, 'What is the story?' Her reply disconcerted me in return. 'Whatever you want it to be.' The
truth was, she didn't know (at least consciously), because she kept
changing the focus as she went along. Motivations pointed like arrows
in all directions. That meant a lot of hacking and rearranging. No
scene remained untouched."[1]

Miss Selznick respected Bagnold's talents and knew that she must tread lightly in aiding in the direction of theme and plot. They worked well together. The artist had someone to guide her creative energies, but her talents lay with language: the craft of playwriting was never easy for her and yet continued to be an exciting challenge. After the play was finished, Bagnold would acknowledge the care and thoroughness with which Selznick had directed her efforts. She felt that Selznick had understood her and had brought out the best in her work.

Other Differences between the Novels and the Plays

The leading characters in the plays are more eccentric, disagreeable, and less believable than the people of the novels. It is difficult to sympathize with Lottie Dundass, the would-be actress, or Edward Walker, the would-be poet. Mrs. St. Maugham of *The Chalk Garden* is close to being unpleasant but is saved by her sense of humor. Rose Portal of *The Last Joke* is a brash, spoiled, insensitive young woman, intent on getting her will. Ferdinand in that play is charming but eccentric in his behavior, a burden to his brother. In *The Chinese Prime Minister* the actress and her husband are sympathetic figures; the son, Tarver, his wife Alice, and Oliver's wife Roxane are often disagreeable, unsympathetic characters, but all are eccentric. In *Call Me Jacky*, aside from Mrs. Basil and a weak Niggie, the characters are not likable or believable people. Especially hateful is Elizabeth, Mrs. Basil's daughter-in-law. In summary, the characters of the plays tend to be artificial, not easy to identify with. These people also find relationships difficult if not impossible.

One has the feeling that the plays, although they contain serious elements, are presented more to entertain than to pose problems. Several are dressed as comedies, but they are not true comedies in the sense that Oscar Wilde's or Noel Coward's or James Barrie's plays are. What the comedies do, however, is reflect the fragmentation and uneasiness of a world in which values are changing. In that sense *The Last Joke, The Chinese Prime Minister,* and *Call Me Jacky/A Matter of Gravity* have some relation to the Theater of the Absurd and are closer to the work of Edward Albee.

The novels and the *Diary* deal with broader issues and more general experience in a serious way. *A Diary without Dates* and *The Happy For-*

eigner deal with the devastation of war, with the protagonists interacting with others outside of their own personal worlds. *Serena Blandish,* a satire, highlights a universal problem in the conflict between the sexes, that of finding a mate (a mate, that is, who can provide a comfortable existence). *National Velvet* presents a fairly realistic panorama of home and community life as Velvet fulfills a dream (but a common fantasy) of competing against the best to win a/the race. *The Squire,* among other things, is about the experience of birth, and *The Loved and Envied* about aging and death and how these processes affect a group of friends.

The plays, on the other hand, tend to deal with a more insulated environment, with individuals trying to cope with their own shortcomings, weaknesses, and desires. In general, the characters live comfortable lives but are beset by frustrations.

Technique

Enid Bagnold enjoyed experimenting with form. When she began writing, the stream-of-consciousness technique had become popular, and she used this impressionistic form in both the true account of *A Diary without Dates* and in her first novel *The Happy Foreigner.* In *Serena Blandish* she reverted to a much older form, the satiric technique of Voltaire and the eighteenth-century philosophical novel; for *National Velvet* she adopted the conventional narrative style popular through the Victorian and Edwardian eras and still popular today. *The Squire* incorporates multiple points of view with a semi-impressionistic style, and for *The Loved and Envied* she chose again the multiple point of view and the omniscient observer in telling the stories of Ruby Maclean and her friends. This last book presented the greatest challenge with its problems of balance and unity. A drastic change came then in the adoption of the drama. She discovered the frustrations of writing in the fairly rigid play form, a form with which she was never comfortable and not at her best. Her greatest successes, therefore, have been with the novel in which she could indulge in narration and description, and revel in the luxury of words, not being overly concerned with plot.

The *Autobiography* is in a class by itself and is perhaps the best book she has written. It, like her first two works, employs an impressionistic style, but a modified one. Her vivid personality and unusual experiences are major reasons for the success of the book, along with the colorful way in which she presents them. An oblique, if poignant, reference to Bagnold's ability to charm is seen in a note from Virginia Woolf to Vita Sackville-West (6 December 1931). Woolf says: "I had a nightmare that you'd discovered say Enid Jones or someone altogether nicer than I am. . . . And now you say you love me—what a relief!"[2]

Bagnold is a superb storyteller. This was true also in her private life. Both Enid and Roderick, apparently, were "talkers," and as she said once, they probably outtalked their children. Her oral storytelling involved the richness of language and love of wit that she displays in her writing. The ability to laugh at herself is important in the effectiveness of her work. She knew her own weaknesses and could present them in a delightful, human way. For instance, one recalls her admitted failure as a "delegator." About this weakness, she says: "I was no delegator. If I had to do something against the grain the only fun was to do it well. It was I who moved the piano while Cutmore looked on. He would have done it but he would have done it wrong. That's the conceit of the non-delegator" (*A*, 204).

One is aware of the tremendous energy that she seems to have had. Irene Selznick comments on this trait and on other qualities as she recalls visits with Bagnold: "Her energy was boundless. . . . She was heroic in her resolve as well as her build, and had the courage of a lion. When it came to detemination, I was fluff compared to Enid. If she couldn't be young, she made a weapon of her age."[3]

The best of her work can be compared favorably with the best in modern literature although she will never be classified as a major writer nor be as famous as her early contemporaries, Katherine Mansfield, Virginia Woolf, or Rebecca West. *National Velvet* and *The Chalk Garden* will continue to be her most noted works, but other writers and persons with an appreciation of style and language will continue to admire or, perhaps, rediscover her talents.

Notes and References

Preface

    1. "Enid Bagnold: Author of 'National Velvet,' " *Times* (London) (1 April 1981), 16.

Chapter One

    1. *Enid Bagnold's Autobiography* (Boston: Little, Brown & Co., 1969) (Issued in 1970), 22; hereafter cited in the text as *A* followed by page number.
    2. Virginia Woolf, *The Letters of Virginia Woolf,* ed. Nigel Nicolson and Joanne Trautmann (vol. 2, 29 January 1918, (New York and London: Harcourt Brace Jovanovich, 1976), Letter #905, 215–16.
    3. Evelyn Waugh, *The Letters of Evelyn Waugh,* ed. Mark Amory (New Haven and New York: Ticknor & Fields, 1980), 247–48.
    4. Ibid., 281.
    5. Ibid.

Chapter Two

    1. E. H. Walton, *"A Diary without Dates,"* New York Times (24 November 1935), 11.
    2. J. S., *"A Dairy without Dates,"* Christian Science Monitor (20 November 1935), 10.
    3. *A Diary without Dates,* (New York: William Morrow & Co., 1935), 5; hereafter cited in the text as *DD*.
    4. David Mitchell, "A Nurse's War," *Times Literary Supplement* (22 September 1978), 1044.
    5. *The Happy Foreigner,* in *The Girl's Journey* (Garden City, N. Y.: Doubleday & Co., 1954), 7; hereafter cited in the text as *HF*.
    6. Arthur Calder-Marshall, Foreword to *The Girl's Journey,* xvii.

Chapter Three

    1. *Serena Blandish: or The Difficulty of Getting Married* (New York: George H. Doran Co., 1925), 7; hereafter page references cited in parentheses in the text.
    2. Voltaire, *Candide,* in *Collected Works of Voltaire* (New York: Greystone Press, n.d.), 119.

3. S. N. Behrman, "Apology to the Author of Serena Blandish," *Three Plays: Serena Blandish, Meteor, The Second Man* (New York: Farrar & Rinehart, 1934), 3.

Chapter Four

1. *National Velvet* (New York: William Morrow & Co., 1975), 148; hereafter cited in the text at *NV*.
2. Kitty Kelley, *Elizabeth Taylor: The Last Star* (New York: Simon & Schuster, 1981), 11.
3. Ibid., 14.
4. *The Squire,* in *The Girl's Journey* (Garden City, N. Y.: Doubleday & Co., 1954), 299; hereafter cited in the text as *S.*
5. Noel Coward, *The Noel Coward Diaries,* ed. Graham Payn & Sheridan Morley (Boston: Little, Brown & Co., 1982), 592.

Chapter Five

1. *The Loved and Envied* (Westport, Conn.: Greenwood Press, 1970), 156, (Copyright 1951, Doubleday & Co.); hereafter page references cited in the text.
2. F. Butcher, "The Loved and Envied," *Chicago Sunday Tribune* (7 January 1951), 3.
3. Anthony West, *New Yorker* (27 January 1951), 86.
4. Robert Kee, *New Statesman and Nation* 41 (10 February 1951); 165.

Chapter Six

1. Coward, *Diaries,* 213.
2. "Lottie Dundass," *New York Times* 19 (22 August 1941); 5.
3. *Lottie Dundass,* in *Theatre* (Garden City, N. Y.: Doubleday & Co., 1951), 26; hereafter cited in the text as *LD.*
4. *Poor Judas* in *Theatre* (Garden City, N. Y.: Doubleday & Co., 1951), 108; hereafter cited in the text as *PJ.*
5. "The Flop," *Atlantic Monthly* (October 1952), 53; page numbers that follow in this chapter refer to this article.

Chapter Seven

1. Kenneth Tynan, " 'The Chalk Garden,' by Enid Bagnold, at the Haymarket," in *Curtains* (New York: Atheneum, 1961), 127.
2. *The Chalk Garden* (New York: Random House, 1956), 6; hereafter page numbers cited in the text.
3. Gerald Weales, "The Madrigal in the Garden," *Tulane Review* (De-

cember 1958, vol. 3, no. 2), in *Laurel British Drama: The Twentieth Century,* ed. Robert W. Corrigan (New York: Dell Publishing Co., 1965), 284.

4. Jack Kroll, "Green Thumb," *Newsweek* (10 May 1982), 89.

5. Ibid.

6. Keith Harper, "Enid Bagnold Talks to Keith Harper," *Guardian* (20 August 1965), 9.

Chapter Eight

1. "The Last Joke," *Four Plays* (Boston: Little, Brown & Co., 1971), 107; hereafter cited in the text as *LJ.*

2. Coward, *Diaries,* 449.

3. *The Chinese Prime Minister,* in *Four Plays* (Little, Brown & Co., 1971), 230; hereafter cited in the text as *CPM.*

4. Walter Kerr, *New York Herald Tribune,* quoted in *Enid Bagnold's Autobiography,* 344.

5. *Call Me Jacky,* in *Four Plays* (Boston: Little, Brown & Co., 1971), 333; hereafter cited in the text as *MG.*

6. *A Matter of Gravity* (New York: Samual French, 1978), v.

7. Martin Gottfried, " 'Gravity' a High for Katharine the Great," *New York Post* (4 February 1976) in *New York Theatre Critics' Reviews* (New York: Theatre Critics Reviews, 1976), 375.

Chapter Nine

1. Irene Mayer Selznick, *A Private View* (New York: Alfred A. Knopf, 1983), 345.

2. Virginia Woolf, *The Letters of Virginia Woolf,* 1929–1931, vol. 4, ed. Nigel Nicolson and Joanne Trautmann (New York and London: Harcourt Brace Jovanovich, 1978), Letter #2477, 6 December 1931, 410.

3. Selznick, *A Private View,* 344.

Selected Bibliography

PRIMARY SOURCES

1. Novels

The Happy Foreigner. London: Heinemann, 1920; New York: Century, 1920.
Serena Blandish: or The Difficulty of Getting Married. London: Heinemann, 1924; New York: Doran, 1925.
National Velvet. London: Heinemann, 1935; New York: Morrow, 1935, 1949, (22d printing, 1975).
The Squire. London: Heinemann, 1938; republished as *The Door of Life*. New York: Morrow, 1938.
The Loved and Envied. London: Heinemann, 1951; Garden City, N. Y.: Doubleday, 1951; Westport, Conn.: Greenwood Press, 1970; London: Chatto & Windus, 1970.

2. Novel Collection

The Girl's Journey. London: Heinemann, 1954; Garden City, N. Y.: Doubleday, 1954. (Includes *The Happy Foreigner* and *The Squire*).

3. Plays

Lottie Dundass. London: Heinemann, 1941.
The Chalk Garden. London: Heinemann, 1956; New York: Random House, 1956.
The Chinese Prime Minister. London: French, 1964; New York: Random House, 1964.
A Matter of Gravity. London: Heinemann, 1978; New York: French, 1978.

4. Play Collections

Two Plays. London: Heinemann, 1951; republished as *Theatre*. Garden City, N. Y.: Doubleday, 1951 (Includes *Lottie Dundass* and *Poor Judas*).
Four Plays. London: Heinemann, 1970; Boston: Little, Brown, 1971 (Includes *The Chalk Garden, The Last Joke, The Chinese Prime Minister,* and *Call Me Jacky*).

5. Nonfiction

A Diary without Dates. London: Heinemann, 1918; Boston: Luce, 1918; New York: William Morrow & Co., 1935. (Reprint.) London: Virago Press, 1978.

Autobiography: From 1889. London: Heinemann, 1969; republished as *Enid Bagnold's Autobiography.* Boston: Little, Brown, 1969 (issued in 1970).

6. Article
"The Flop." *Atlantic Monthly* 4 (October 1952): 53–57.

7. Children's Book
Alice and Thomas and Jane. London: Heinemann, 1930; New York: Knopf, 1931.

8. Poems
The Sailing Ships and Other Poems. London: Heinemann, 1917.

9. Letters
Letters to Frank Harris and Other Friends. Edited by R. P. Lister. Andoversford, Gloucestershire: Whittington Press/Heinemann, 1980.

10. Adaptation
National Velvet (play). In *Embassy Successes II 1945–46.* London: Low, Marston, 1946.

11. Translation
Alexander of Asia. By Princess Marthe Bibesco. London: Heinemann, 1935.

SECONDARY SOURCES

Not much has been written about Enid Bagnold apart from brief discussions in reference works and book and play reviews. There are no extensive bibliographies other than the usual listings of primary sources. The works included here are representative of materials available.

1. Biography
Aronson, Steven M. L. "Irene Selznick." *House & Garden,* July 1983, 14, 16, 20. In this interview Irene Selznick speaks of Enid and Roderick Jones and her visits with them as they worked on *The Chalk Garden.*
"Enid Bagnold." *Who's Who in the Theatre.* Ian Herbert, editor, with C. Baxter and R. E. Finlay, p. 35. 17th ed. Detroit: Gale Research Company, 1981. Brief listing, gives only essential facts.
Gale, John. "Just the Type for H. G. Wells." *Observer* (London), 26 October 1969, 23. An interview with Enid Bagnold at home in Rottingdean. He refers to her as one of the most elegant and concise writers of the theater.

Harper, Keith. "Enid Bagnold talks to Keith Harper." *Guardian*, 20 August 1965, 9. An interview with Enid Bagnold at home. He describes her in her surroundings and there is some discussion of her work.

Kunitz, Stanley J., ed. "Enid Bagnold." *Twentieth Century Authors*, 36–37. New York: H. W. Wilson Company, 1955. Brief biographical sketch with list of her works.

Selznick, Irene Mayer. "The Chalk Garden." *A Private View*, 341–53. New York: Alfred A. Knopf, 1983. This chapter is devoted to her experiences with the production of *The Chalk Garden* and her working relationship with Enid Bagnold.

2. Critical Discussions

Calder-Marshall, Arthur. Foreword to *The Girl's Journey*. Garden City, New York: Doubleday & Co., 1954. An excellent discussion of the characteristics of her novels, noting the heavy autobiographical influence and also the variety in the style and kinds of works. He concentrates on *The Happy Foreigner* and *The Squire*.

"Enid Bagnold: Author of 'National Velvet.' " *Times* (London) 1 April 1981, 16. Obituary. Discusses briefly her writing career and her most famous works. Commends her on the sharpening and refinement of language.

Gidez, Richard B. "Enid Bagnold." *Dictionary of Literary Biography: British Dramatists since World War II*, vol. 13, pt. 1: A-L, 33–39. Detroit: Gale Research Company, 1982. Includes a good discussion of the plays. Mentions Walter Kerr and Brooks Atkinson as critics who have suggested that Bagnold is more at ease with fiction. Comments on the lack of action in the plays but appreciates the "stimulating conversation, exciting ideas, and mature understanding."

Leech, Michael. "Enid Bagnold." In *Contemporary Novelists*, edited by James Vinson, 74–77. New York: St. Martin's Press, 1976. A brief but positive view of the prose works; considers her a remarkable novelist but says that much can also be learned about her from her frustrating passion for the theater.

McNaughton, Howard. "Enid Bagnold." In *Great Writers of the English Language: Dramatists*, edited by James Vinson, 25–26. New York: Macmillan Press Ltd., 1979. Comments on her works, saying that the early plays "reveal an uncertain handling of a somewhat fanciful story-line which would be more acceptable in prose form"; praises *The Chalk Garden;* finds the later plays not as effective but points out that their literary sophistication insures popularity as plays to be read.

Young, B. A. "Enid Bagnold." In *Contemporary Dramatists*, edited by James Vinson, 57–61. New York: St. Martin's Press, 1977. Quotes some of Enid Bagnold's comments on writing, also Walter Kerr's review of *The Chinese Prime Minister*. A good discussion of the plays. Says *The Chinese Prime Minister* should not be neglected. Says *The Chalk Garden* initiated a mandarin style that characterizes her last four plays. Praises *The Chalk Garden* and its larger-than-life people.

3. Selected Book Reviews

a. *A Diary without Dates* (1918) (Reprints 1935, 1978)

Boston Transcript, 23 November 1935, 5. Says this is much more than a war book. Among its merits are its style, its charmingly selected words, its sincerity, and its delicacy of understanding.

J. S. *Christian Science Monitor,* 20 November 1935, 10. Says book shows promise of an unusual power of writing and that the writer herself is more interesting than the people she describes, that she saw things that others only felt.

Mitchell, David. "A Nurse's War." *Times Literary Supplement,* 22 September 1978, 1044. Praises the book; says it is artfully constructed, that it captures atmosphere of the hospital with notable economy, and that such accounts have produced the most poignant impressions of the time.

Walton, E. H. *New York Times,* 24 November 1935, 11. Says that after two decades and a plethora of war literature the book is still worth reading and reprinting; also that it communicates emotion directly and poignantly.

b. *The Happy Foreigner* (1920)

Calder-Marshall, Arthur. Foreword to *The Girl's Journey.* London: Heinemann, 1954; Garden City, N. Y.: Doubleday, 1954. Says that her points are made by minute description rather than analysis and that weather and landscape are as important characters as the people; finds her ending more satisfactory than Hemingway's in *A Farewell to Arms;* calls Bagnold a pre-Christian writer, a stoic; says her books are deeply happy and full of joy because they accept rather than deny sadness.

Times Literary Supplement, 1 July 1920, 422. Praises the novel; says Bagnold has captured the desolation and the spirit of the time within a few words, that she seems to see it all with a personal detachment blended with an intense sympathy for others; the experiences become vivid; says she has splendid equipment for a novelist.

c. *Serena Blandish* (1924)

Behrman, S. N. "To the Author of Serena Blandish An Apology." Foreword to *Three Plays: Serena Blandish, Meteor, The Second Man.* New York: Farrar & Rinehart, 1934. Praises the novel; calls it innocent, yet insidious; wishes he could have written it. Apologizes for not having been able to transfer the novel to the stage as successfully as he had wished; realizes that the language of the book is essential to its effectiveness.

Times Literary Supplement, 18 December 1924, 868. Positive review. Says the difficulty of getting married has never been treated with greater freedom or completer knowledge, a brilliant tract for the times; subject never handled so firmly or precisely.

d. *National Velvet* (1935)

Gannett, Lewis. *New York Herald Tribune,* 26 April 1935, 15. " 'National Velvet' is a book to buy, to read, to remember and to talk about and to keep instead of lending."

Morley, Christopher. *Saturday Review of Literature* 12 (4 May 1935): 6. Very positive review; says that for those who can ride the flying trapeze of fancy, this is a masterpiece.

Times Literary Supplement, 4 April 1935, 226. Calls it a story that is at the same time breathlessly exciting and a delightful character study.

W. K. R. *Christian Science Monitor,* 26 April 1935, 18. Says the account of the race is glorious but praises more the character portrayals. Calls it a fantastic, preposterous, and delightful tale.

e. *The Squire* (1938)

Calder-Marshall, Arthur. Foreword to *The Girl's Journey.* London: Heinemann, 1954; Garden City, N. Y.: Doubleday, 1954. Calls *The Squire* an "autumnal book, rich with the harvest of a full life"; says it is much more complicated than it seems. There is not much of plot and no suspense, but there is solid characterization. The below-the-surface meditation on human existence is an essential element, he says.

Times Literary Supplement, 15 October 1938, 659. Positive review; finds the book out of the ordinary, intensely subjective, more for women; little plot but treatment of personal relationships is one of the author's triumphs; comments that there is repetition but much to give delight and provoke thought.

f. *The Loved and Envied* (1951)

Brown, C. M. *Saturday Review of Literature* 34 (6 January 1951): 30. Says this is a truly remarkable novel about a truly remarkable woman. Bagnold is witty, worldly, and wise and the book displays her qualities at their best.

Butcher, Fanny. *Chicago Sunday Tribune,* 7 January 1951, 3. Praises the book highly; says she has never read a book more understanding or enchantingly written about the aged and their philosophies; this is not a typical book about the subject.

Lerman, Leo. *New York Times,* 31 December 1950, 5. Praises the intricate design of the book; says that it is not merely a novel of the life of the wealthy but "a charting of the death of many hearts."

Ross, Mary. *New York Herald Tribune Book Review,* 31 December 1950, 3.
Says although there is little action in the book, it holds one's attention
and that Bagnold has done a perceptive and distinguished job in making the characters credible human beings.

Times Literary Supplement, 26 January 1951, 49. A negative view; acknowledges that several distinguished critics hailed the book; finds, beneath
the polished surface, sentimentality and snobbery.

West, Anthony. *New Yorker,* 26 (27 January 1951): 86. Praises the book
and the way it creates an atmosphere of maturity, also the skill with
which Bagnold has created adolescent rebellion and its effect on the
mother/daughter relationship. His one objection is that, like so many
British writers, she "dearly loves a lord."

g. *Enid Bagnold's Autobiography* (1969)

Bozeman, Mary. *Library Journal* 95 (15 September 1970):2906. Says her
humanity shines through every page; comments on her razor-sharp
mind and acute observations of the human condition. Her overall opinion is that Bagnold's book is "a treasure—not just the story of a life
but an engrossing experience not to be missed."

Houghton, Norris. *Saturday Review of Literature* 53 (26 September
1970):30. Appreciates the book but says she can judge better the part
dealing with the theater. Finds that her accounts of stage triumphs and
failures are packed with so much truth and illustrated by so many telling incidents that the book should be devoured by all aspiring dramatists.

Sayre, Nora. *New York Times Book Review,* 30 August 1970, 4. Finds this
a splendid memoir, full of energy; Bagnold's friends and acquaintances
"leap to life in a few words," and one wishes for more stories.

Times Literary Supplement, 4 December 1969, 1376. A lukewarm review; finds
her method of storytelling cool, amusing but detached; remarks that
the author does not come to nearly such close quarters with herself as
in the novels. Says her talents are great but not superlative.

4. Selected Play Reviews

a. *The Chalk Garden* (1956)

Atkinson, Brooks. "The Chalk Garden." *New York Times,* sec. 2, 13 November 1955, 1. Says that this play is witty in the literary tradition of
Congreve, that the lines are carefully polished; called it courageous,
subtle, and detached, evidence of a stimulating mind at work; says that
the play asks as many questions as it answers but that they are all original and intelligent.

Hewes, Henry. "The Accents of Truth." *Saturday Review of Literature* 38 (12 November 1955):24. Gives strong praise; says the play "lives in the intangibles of heart and human will," and that it is extremely poetic and witty, a hypnotic piece of theater.

Kroll, Jack. "Green Thumb." *Newsweek,* 10 May, 1982, 89. Says the play reflects Bagnold's tremendously vigorous and attractive personality and that it echoes the work of Congreve, Wilde, and Shaw, of every British master of graceful epigram, "significant witticism, sagacious irony"; finds it a grown-up, sophisticated play.

Tynan, Kenneth. " 'The Chalk Garden,' by Enid Bagnold at the Haymarket." In *Curtains,* 127–28. New York: Atheneum, 1961. This review has become a classic. Says the play "may well be the finest artificial comedy to have flowed from an English pen since the death of Congreve." He comments on the verbal precision.

Weales, Gerald. "The Madrigal in the Garden." In *Laurel British Drama: The Twentieth Century,* edited by Robert W. Corrigan, 283–93. New York: Dell Publishing Co., 1965. The most complete and the best essay so far on *The Chalk Garden,* a classic; praising the play, he discusses the critical reviews, the dialogue, the characterization, the theme, and the possible religious aspects.

b. *The Chinese Prime Minister* (1964)

McCarten, John. "Durable Dame." *New Yorker* 39 (11 January 1964):69. Calls this a fine drawing room comedy; says Bagnold has a way with dialogue, but play becomes a bit murky in act 2 and is not sure if at end the author's case had a sound base.

"70 Wanting to be 17." *Time* 83 (10 January 1964):52. Says this succeeds because of Bagnold's love of language and the excellent actress (Margaret Leighton) playing the lead. Contends that old age is what the playwright meant to write about, but that "unwittingly her play is about the youth complex."

Taubman, Howard. "Chinese Prime Minister." *New York Times,* 3 January 1964, 14. Refers to *The Chalk Garden* as model of elliptical humor and wisdom; says Bagnold is writing again with civilized wit and mature understanding; this is not a conventional comedy of manners but uses form to compose "a delicious fantasy." Finds it short on action but with stimulating talk and spirited minds.

Young, B. A. "Bagnold's 'Minister' is Staged in London." *New York Times,* 21 May 1965, 21. Says the combination of Enid Bagnold and Dame Edith Evans works out happily; in place of plot, Miss Bagnold has created "elegant, civilized conversation," and Dame Edith's part suits her perfectly.

c. *A Matter of Gravity* (1978)

Barnes, Clive. "Hepburn is Center of 'Gravity.' " *New York Times*, 5 February 1976, 25. He is not sure that he understood the play which enshrines the star (Katharine Hepburn); finds it full of "cross-currents of motivation and whirlpools of thought." Calls the characters unlikely and apart from Mrs. Basil, disagreeable. Objects also to the epigrams and ponderous sayings.

Beaufort, John. "That Hepburn Magic Wins Broadway Again." *Christian Science Monitor*, 6 February 1976 (in *New York Theatre Critics' Reviews*, 1976, 377). Calls it a strange and whimsical play with unlikely characters and patchwork plotting but it has a certain "gallantry of its own."

Gottfried, Martin. " 'Gravity' a High for Katharine the Great." *New York Post*, 4 February 1976 (in *New York Theatre Critics' Reviews*, 1976, 375). The only really positive review. Finds the play written with grace in pursuit of intelligence. The sociological points are confused, he says, but it is a play of charm and wisdom. Praises the dialogue and the wit.

Michener, Charles. "Comedy of Bad Manners." *Newsweek*, 16 February 1976, 77. Calls it a British comedy of manners which in essence means rudeness. Says Bagnold has more epigrams in her arsenal than Wilde ever rejected.

Index